INSIGHT POCKET GUIDES

S

CW01018633

APA PUBLICATIONS

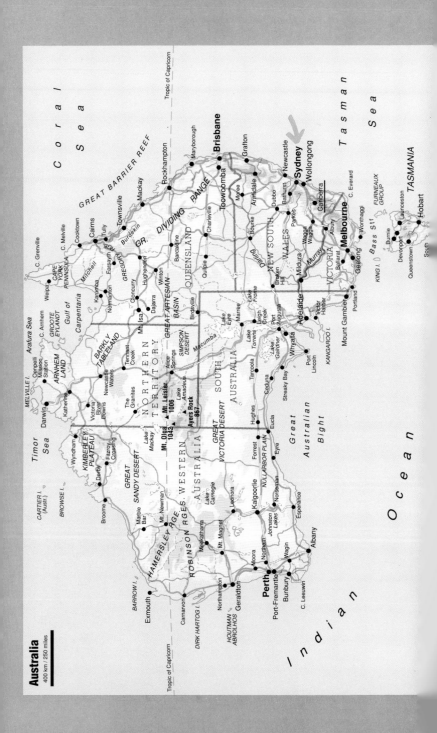

Australia

400 km / 250 miles

Guten Tag!

A melting pot of Asian, Oceanian, European and American cultures. An exciting metropolis famed for its sparkling blue harbour and its dramatic Opera House. Now add yet another reason to visit Sydney as it prepares to welcome the world as host city of the year 2000 Olympics.

In these pages, two of Insight's Australian correspondents help enrich your experience of the city. Both are Sydney-based travel writers and photographers who've made individual odysseys overseas and returned, not because coming home was inevitable but because Sydney is such a great city to live in. Their carefully-crafted itineraries are designed to cover all the must-see attractions as well as some of the lesser-known sights in the shortest possible time.

David McGonigal left the city and Australia in 1976 only to return four years later to make it his home. His love affair with this warm and wonderful harbourside city endures to this day. 'Few would contest Sydney's claim as one of the world's most scenically spectacular cities, a shimmering delight of sunlight off water and golden beaches', he contends. This Sydneysider's unabashed awe for the city is obvious in the itineraries he has put together.

John Borthwick had heaps of fun researching and writing this book. In doing so he rediscovered the city, or as he puts it: 'became a tourist at home'. Borthwick recognises that much has been made about Sydney being the 'the best address on earth'. For him, this simply translates to being at home. That home and Sydney are synonymous is something Borthwick counts as a definite blessing. His itineraries reveal an insider's view of Sydney.

Hans Höfer
Publisher, Insight Guides

C O N T E N T S

Pages 2/3: celebrating the nation's 200th birthday at Sydney Harbour

Excursions

These excursions are ideal for those who wish to get
out of the city and experience some of the raw,
natural beauty that Australia is famous for.

Shopping, Dining & Nightlife

In this back part of the book are our recommended
selections of where to shop, eat and stay up late **80–91**

Calendar of Events

A listing of what's worth watching out for in an event-
packed Sydney year...**92**

Practical Information

All the essential background information for your
visit to Sydney, from taxis to tipping, customs to
consulates, plus a list of recommended hotels............**93–103**

Maps

*Pages 8/9:
'Sydney Explorer'
– a cheap and
quick way to cover
the city sights*

R 153

HISTORY & CULTURE

Sydney is at once one of the oldest and one of the newest cities in the world. It is estimated that the first inhabitants arrived here some 50,000 years ago. However, despite the development of an intricate social fabric, those early Aborigines imposed little change – and certainly no damage – on the landscape. All that changed a little over 200 years ago when the British Government decided to locate an open-air prison here. Since then, Sydney has grown to fill much of the available land between the sea and the Blue Mountains, some 60km (37 miles) inland.

Beginnings

When the first Aborigines arrived in what is now Sydney, the harbour did not exist: it was a dry valley about 10km (6 miles) inland. The earliest stone tools found in the region date back more than 45,000 years. About 10,000 years ago, the ice caps started to melt and coastlines altered until the seas stabilised at their present level, about 6,000 years before the first Europeans arrived.

Despite what most people think, Captain James Cook did not discover Australia. By 29 April 1770, when the 41-year-old British

The British declared this 'the finest harbour in the world' in 1788

Royal Navy officer sailed the *Endeavour* into a sheltered bay where he noted a 'fine meadow', the north, south and west coasts of the continent had already been explored by Dutch, Portuguese and Spanish navigators over the previous two centuries. However, none had ventured to as far as the east coast, which Captain Cook followed from about the present New South Wales-Victoria border to Botany Bay, south of today's Sydney and to the tip of Queensland at Cape York. The *Endeavour* spent a week in Botany Bay but the crew had little

Kurnell – where Cook first stepped ashore

contact with the 3,000 local Aborigines. Cook noted that 'all they seemed to want was for us to be gone'.

At first, the English government had little use for the land which Cook had claimed in the name of the crown. However, the American Declaration of Independence in 1776 stopped transportation of convicts to the southern plantations and penal settlements such as Georgia. With that door closed, English prisons soon filled and rotting hulks of ships on the Thames River took the overflow. In August 1786, Lord Sydney (Thomas Townsend), the British Home Secretary, instructed the Admiralty to arrange for Botany Bay to receive a fleet of marines and convicts. This marked the inauspicious start of a new nation.

First Settlement

On 13 May 1787, a fleet of 11 ships sailed from Portsmouth, and eventually laboured into Botany Bay, some 22,500km (14,000 miles) away on 20 January 1788. An inadequate water supply there led Captain Arthur Phillip into Port Jackson (which James Cook had merely noted in passing) and found what he declared to be 'the finest harbour in the world'. The whole colony moved to what Captain Phillip named 'Sydney Cove'. On Saturday 26 January 1788, the Union Jack flew for the first time over the tiny settlement of 568 male and 191 female convicts, plus 200 marines accompanied by 27 wives and 25 children.

There was every likelihood during those first years that the new colony would starve and founder. The Aborigines kept away, so the

Captain Cook

A historical re-enactment of Sydney's early days

settlers had to find out for themselves how to survive in a land far different from any they knew. By mid-1790, the colony, now known as 'New South Wales', was saved from starvation only when a supply ship arrived. Soon afterwards, the Second Fleet sailed into port in terrible condition: 267 convicts had died on the voyage and a further 124 died soon after their arrival.

The settlers clung to the foreshores of Sydney Cove for a long time. Captain Phillip, now the governor, devised a town plan but everyone ignored it, bringing about the haphazard street grid of present-day Sydney. Phillip was followed by governors Hunter, King and then Bligh. The latter came to Sydney on his first appointment after the famed mutiny on the *Bounty*.

Beginnings of Nationhood

The inspired 12-year term of Governor Lachlan Macquarie from 1810 to 1821 took New South Wales from foundling colony to fledgling community. Sydney continues to bear the indelible stamp of Macquarie and his principal architect, the forger, convict and genius Francis Greenway. It was Macquarie who established a designated street width (with footpaths) and demolished buildings which stood in its way. Greenway-designed churches that survive today include St James' in the city, St Matthew's at Windsor and St Luke's in Liverpool. Governor Macquarie pardoned Greenway after he designed Hyde Park Barracks (still standing in Macquarie Street), but Greenway's fortunes declined after his patron departed: Commissioner Bigge considered his work 'too grand for an infant colony'.

Governor Macquarie also gave Australia its name when, in 1817, he first used the word 'Australia' in his correspondence. The word came from the earlier expression '*Terra Australis*', meaning simply, south land.

Although it took 24 years to find a way across the Blue Mountains to the pasture lands of the west, the population of Sydney increased rapidly when the convict population was boosted by the arrival of free settlers. Even so, by 1820, the town of Sydney barely covered 2½ sq km (1sq mile). The first street in Australia was the bullock track that became George Street and the first road leading out of Sydney was built to Parramatta in 1794.

Smallpox killed half the Aboriginal population before the colony was two years old and within 50 years of white settlement, fewer than 300 Aborigines remained in the region. Even so, many Sydney suburbs were given Aboriginal names.

Convict migration ceased in 1840. A total of 83,000 convicts had been sent to New South Wales and most stayed there to make a home in the colony. Charles Darwin, the author of *The Origin of Species*, visited Sydney in 1836 and concluded that 'as a real system of reform it has failed... but as a means of making men outwardly honest – of converting vagabonds most useless in one hemisphere into active citizens of another, and thus giving birth to a new and splendid country – a grand centre of civilisation – it has succeeded to a degree perhaps unparalleled in history'.

Gold Rush

Sydney town was declared the City of Sydney in July 1842. Less than a decade later, Australia's first publicised gold discovery was made near Bathurst, on the other side of the Blue Mountains, by E H Hargraves. Hargraves returned from the California gold fields claiming that they reminded him of parts of New South Wales. Despite general ridicule, he proceeded from Sydney to Bathurst with an acquaintance and announced that they were standing on gold. His first panful of dirt produced gold and he declared: 'Here it is. This is a memorable day in the history of New South Wales. I shall be a baronet, and you will be knighted, and my old horse will be stuffed, put in a glass case and sent to the British Museum!' He was right about the gold but wrong about the rest – the remainder of his life was uneventful until he died in 1891.

Hargraves' discovery started a rush that boosted the fortunes of Sydney: its population nearly doubled in 10 years, from 54,000 in 1851 to 96,000 in 1861. By 1885, the main city streets were paved with wooden blocks, finally removing the dust pall which had plagued the city for years. Buildings befitting a city of Victoria's Britain were built, including the Town Hall in 1889, the Customs House in 1887 and

...iginal didgeridoo players

the Art Gallery. In 1895, Samuel Clements (Mark Twain) visited Sydney and declared it 'an English city with American trimmings'. The same accusation is still made today.

Australian Federation

On 1 January 1901, the Commonwealth of Australia came into existence. Thousands of people poured into Centennial Park in Sydney to watch the swearing-in of Australia's first Governor General. By this time, Sydney was a vibrant city with an established literary and arts movement: it had come a long way from the days when life was merely a matter of survival.

At the same time, Sydney was recovering from the major depression of 1892. The Australian colonies largely traded themselves out of trouble by greatly expanding the areas under wheat cultivation. A more immediate urban problem was an outbreak of bubonic plague which killed 112 people in Sydney in 1900. The direct result was that the slums of the Rocks area had a long overdue clean-up.

World Wars

On 18 August 1914, the Australian Naval and Military Expeditionary Force left Sydney for German New Guinea, becoming the first Australian troops to join World War I. During the next four years, some 60,000 of the 330,000 Australian troops who served overseas died.

The post-war period was a time of innovation – Sydney's underground railway opened in 1926 and the England-Australia Telephone Service commenced in 1930 – but this was followed by the Great Depression. The debate on how to tackle the debilitating level of unemployment developed into a class war: the Labor government of Premier Jack Lang against the right-wing New Guard. When the Sydney Harbour Bridge was opened in March 1932, Captain de Groot of the paramilitary New Guard slashed the ribbon with his sword before Jack Lang could ceremonially cut it.

In 1921, there were 30,000 cars registered in New South Wales: this figure had risen to more than 625,000 in 1961 and 1.4 million in 1975. A casualty of the motor car era was the Sydney tram. Although the expression 'shoot through like a Bondi tram' is still occasionally used, the last tram completed its run in 1961. However, it wasn't only the automobile population that grew dramatically. From half a million at the turn of the century, Sydney's population passed the 1 million mark before 1931, and 2 million before 1961. It currently stands at over 3½ million.

Customs House's imperial insignia

Open-air jazz, Circular Quay

Changing Populations and Attitudes

After World War II, the stream of new arrivals continued as many left Europe to seek a new life overseas. Over 75 percent of Sydney's population growth between 1947 and 1971 came from European immigrants, especially Italians and Greeks and their Australian-born children. This and subsequent influxes, mainly from Asia, changed Sydney from a very insular colonial outpost into a multi-cultural cosmopolitan city.

The tallest building in Sydney before World War II was 11-storeys high. In 1961, the AMP insurance company completed its 26-storey building on Circular Quay. Crowds flocked to marvel at the view from the top of this building. By 1968, the vogue rooftop eyrie was the 50-floor circular tower of Australia Square. The highest construction in Sydney to date – at 305m (1,000ft) – is the Sydney Tower on top of Centrepoint.

After the soul-searching Vietnam War moratorium marches of the late 1960s and early 1970s, Sydney appeared to have slipped into social somnolence during most of the 70s. The 70s slipped into the 80s and the age of the yuppie, when lives became 'lifestyles'.

Sydney awakened on 26 January 1988 to greet the dawn of the third century of white settlement. The city had come of age. The 90s have seen a new mood of enduring optimism. In 1992, the new harbour car tunnel opened – the first new harbour crossing for several decades. In 1994, the city gained a much-needed third runway at the international airport. And, in April 1995, a new state Labor government was elected on a wide policy platform of reform. But most of all, the event that has defined this decade took place in September 1993, when it was announced that Sydney was to be the host city of the 2000 Olympic Games. Besides triggering an extensive building programme across the city, this choice of a British settlement in Asia with a cosmopolitan population and an international perspective to host the games that will begin the third millennium seems a fitting one.

15

Historical Highlights

50,000 BC (approximate) The first Aborigines arrive.

29 April 1770 Captain James Cook sails the *Endeavour* into Botany Bay.

August 1786 Lord Sydney, the Home Secretary, instructs the British Admiralty to arrange what was to be dubbed a 'colony of thieves' at Botany Bay.

13 May 1787 A fleet of ships sail from Portsmouth to Botany Bay.

20 January 1788 The First Fleet arrives in Botany Bay.

26 January 1788 The new colony moves to Sydney Cove.

1794 The first road leading out of Sydney is built to Parramatta.

1804 Irish prisoners rise against the government at Vinegar Hill.

1810–1821 Governor Macquarie takes New South Wales from colony to fledgling community. Sydney's population in 1810 numbers 6,156.

1817 Macquarie first uses the word 'Australia' in official correspondence.

1820 Sydney's land area extends to 2½sq km (1sq mile).

1828 Sydney's population numbers 10,815.

1832 Free settlers are offered assisted passage to the new colony.

1840 Transportation of convicts to New South Wales ceases (a total of 83,000 convicts were sent).

July 1842 Sydney town declared the City of Sydney.

1851 The first publicised gold discovery in Australia is made near Bathurst by E H Hargraves.

1861 Sydney's population has doubled in 10 years to reach 96,000.

1890–1891 Labour strikes cripple the colony.

1892 Sydney and the other Australian colonies experience a major depression.

1889 Sydney Town Hall opens.

1900 Outbreak of bubonic plague kills 112. The Rocks has a long overdue clean-up.

1 January 1901 Australian Federation. Australia's first governor-general, Lord Hopeton, is sworn in.

1909 Australia's first aerial flight takes place at Narrabeen Beach.

1912 Australia's first air race between Sydney and Parramatta.

18 August 1914 First Australian troops to join World War I leave Sydney for German New Guinea.

1926 The much-awaited Sydney underground railway opens.

1930 England-Australia Telephone Service starts, putting Sydney in direct voice contact with London.

1931 Sydney's population passes the 1 million mark.

March 1932 The Sydney Harbour Bridge opens.

May 1942 Three Japanese midget submarines enter Sydney Harbour and torpedo a ferry.

1960 Eight-year-old Graham Thorne has the dubious distinction of becoming Australia's first kidnap-ransom victim.

1961 The last Sydney tram finishes its run.

1966 Australia's currency changes from pounds, shillings and pence to decimal dollars and cents.

1973 Sydney Opera House is officially opened by Queen Elizabeth II. Patrick White receives the Nobel Prize for Literature.

1975 Labor Prime Minister Gough Whitlam is dismissed amid great controversy. People take to the streets in protest.

1979 The long-awaited Eastern Suburbs railway opens.

24 October 1980 Multicultural television station SBS begins transmission in Sydney and Melbourne.

1981 Pat O'Shane, Australia's first Aboriginal law graduate, becomes the first woman to head a New South Wales government department.

26 January 1988 Celebration of Australia's bicentenary.

August 1992 The Sydney Harbour Tunnel opens.

September 1993 Formal agreement that Sydney will host the 2000 Olympic Games.

November 1994 A third runaway opens at the airport, amid great controversy over aircraft noise.

April 1995 A state Labor government elected.

Right, Governor William Bligh

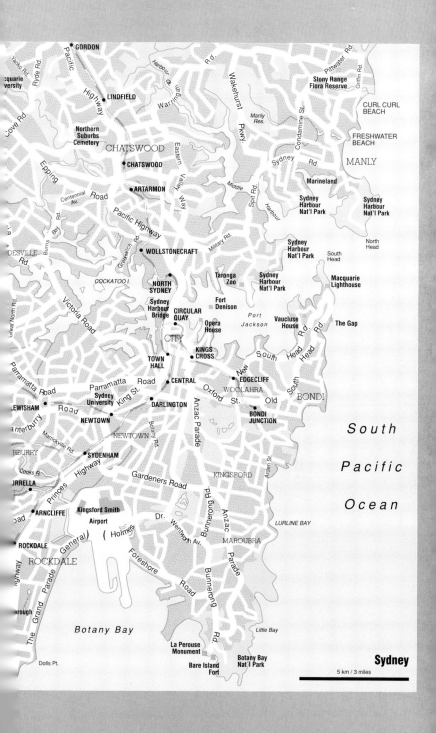

Sydney

5 km / 3 miles

Day Itineraries

DAY 1

This might seem like a very full day – but why not try? There's a taste of Sydney Harbour's distant and near history, the shopping-spree Central Business District as well as good eats in Oxford Street – plus a naughty Kings Cross evening of scarlet libidos.

City Highlights

800 m / 0.5 miles

1 Wharf Theatre Restaurant
2 Lord Nelson Hotel
3 Garrison Church
4 Argyle Arts Centre
5 Clocktower Centre
6 Pier One
7 Earth Exchange
8 Overseas Passenger Teminal
9 Cadmans Cottage
10 Circular Quay
11 Park Hyatt Hotel
12 Hero of Waterloo
13 Museum of Contemporary Art
14 Opera House
15 Customs House
16 Pyramid Glasshouse
17 Nikko Hotel
18 Skygarden
19 Sydney Tower
20 Queen Victoria Bldg.
21 Burdekin Hotel
22 Albury Hotel
23 Acad. Twin Cinema
24 Town Hall
25 Strand Arcade

To meet Sydney on its own terms, do it early, say by 8 or 9am. First slip on some good walking shoes, then hail a taxi for **'Mrs Macquarie's Point'** at the end of Art Gallery Road. The view from here affords a fine profile of the Opera House, tiny Fort Denison and the north side of the harbour. Hordes of Japanese honeymooners come here to be photographed. Have a chuckle

Sydney Opera House at Bennelong Point

at the queue of tour groups posing before the operatic backdrop.

It's a short walk around Farm Cove (so named because this was the site of the first European farm on the continent) to the Opera House along the shoreline path which skirts the **Royal Botanic Gardens** (open daily during daylight hours, tel: 92318111). Wander through the picturesque 30ha (74 acres) of duck ponds, statues and Australian and imported flora, and check out the lush tropical plants in the **Pyramid Glasshouse**. At any time of day this is a great spot for a picnic or for smooching, although it does close respectably at dusk.

The **Sydney Opera House**, sitting on **Bennelong Point** like a great crystal, is immediately recognisable. It has been likened to a basket of washing on a windy day. Or a typewriter full of oyster shells. Housing theatres, restaurants, a cinema and more, its roof shells soar to 67m (220ft) and are covered by 1 million tiles (see *Pick & Mix 2, page 40*). Wander around at will, but do make sure you see the inside of this wonder.

Circular Quay puppeteer

A covered walkway runs from the Opera House around Sydney Cove to **Circular Quay** (which is actually rectangle), where the 'First Fleet' settlers landed in 1788. 'The Quay' is the hub of Sydney's ferries, and a motley group of buskers, tourists and commuters. The only surviving historic building is the 1885 **Customs House**. Numerous places to snack, drink or lunch can detain you here. Watch out for a number of avaricious cafes at the entrance to the ferry wharves, which charge enormous sums for very ordinary food.

Continue strolling in the general direc-

tion of the Harbour Bridge, around the waterfront, past the Museum of Contemporary Art and the Overseas Passenger Terminal and into The Rocks.

This most historic (as well as touristic) precinct of Sydney, **The Rocks** is a huge sink for both your money and time. This area (named simply after the rocky peninsula on which it was built) was the birthplace of European settlement in Australia, and its once haphazard collection of hovels, brothels, wharves and bond stores have now been scrubbed up into boutiques, craft galleries and restaurants. It is best explored by throwing the map away somewhere around the **Argyle Centre** (entrance at 18 Argyle Street) and getting lost in alleys like Suez Canal (formerly 'Sewer's Canal') and Nurses Walk.

There are a number of sights in The Rocks. The 1816 **Cadman's Cottage** (Monday to Friday 9.30am–4pm, Saturday and Sunday 11am–4pm) at 110 George Street – just inland of the Overseas Passenger Terminal and north of a bronze, mutiny-proof statue of Governor William Bligh, is the oldest extant residence in Australia. Despite renovations, it looks its age.

Further along George Street, at No 104, **The Rocks Visitors' Centre** (open daily 9am–5pm, tel: 92474972) will provide you with current information and maps of the area and its surroundings. Up Argyle Street, through the sandstone chasm of the 'Argyle Cut', the **Lord Nelson Hotel** (corner of Kent Street), the oldest hotel in Sydney, will provide the beer, while the 1844 **Garrison Church** deals with spirits of the heavenly sort. The **Hero of Waterloo** (81 Windmill Street) is another historic watering hole, and on a Sunday afternoon has the world's oldest pub band, a bunch of tuneful octo-

The bridge from The Rocks

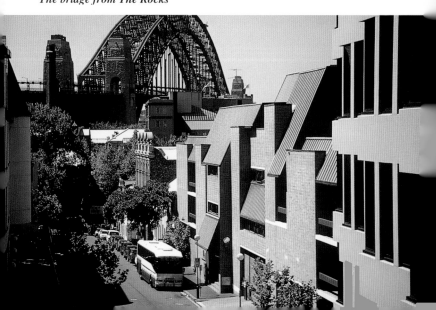

Sydney Cove restaurants: dining with history

genarians (think of them as U82). A pub 'counter lunch' at any pub is an unpretentious meal and a chance to meet the locals.

A walk around the western shore of Sydney Cove brings you to past the Park Hyatt Hotel to the **Earth Exchange** mining museum at 18 Hickson Road, tel: 92512422 (see *Pick & Mix 3, page 44*); **Dawes Point** (where the sky is blocked by the imposing bulk of the Harbour Bridge); **Pier One**, with more fast (and slow) foods and grand harbour vistas; and finally to the much-awarded **Wharf Theatre and Restaurant** (see *Eating Out*) at Pier Four.

The rest of the day is at your own leisure. If shopping is at the top of your list of priorities, read on. The bubonic plague may have disappeared from The Rocks more than a century ago, but no one is safe from the contagion of opals, boomerangs, designer junk and other items of antipodean excess baggage. The **Crafts Centre** (88 George Street) has Australian-made crafts and gifts, while the **Argyle Centre** and the **Clocktower Centre** are warrens of trinket galleries, opal shops and Australiana clothing stores. George Street from the Quay to Harbour Bridge is one endless boutique of opal jewellery, T-shirts and lambswool everything. Australian artist Ken Done has painted himself permanently into the corner of the Rocks with a gallery at 1 Hickson Road.

Before you spend all day and all your precious dollars here, grab a cab for the short ride south to the **Queen Victoria Building (QVB)**, occupying a whole block of George Street to the harbour side of the Town Hall. Refurbished in 1986, this is the Cinderella of Sydney architecture: an exquisite 19th-century grand design in stone and stained glass. Almost 200 quality shops line the mezzanine galleries. It's a great wander, has a silly clock on the ceiling and a stupendous Chinese jade carriage on the top floor, and on the

'Skydining' at Skygarden

lowest level, an 'Eat Street' for reasonably priced fast food with limited seating. Leave the QVB's Victorian grandeur by tunnelling out of its lower depths to the Town Hall railway station or any other street exit. It is always a surprise to see where you'll pop up.

In the next block north (towards the harbour) is the late 19th-century **Strand Arcade** (412 George Street). With its tiered mezzanines and ironwork, this is another venerable, still beautiful, architectural gem. The building connects George and Pitt streets (between King and Market streets). Quality jewellers, watchmakers and fashion designers trade cheek-by-jowl with coffee houses and gift shops, but for many visitors the real attraction is the building itself. A visit here is not just a re-run of the QVB – it's a reminder of Australia's early links with London.

Walk through the Strand Arcade and emerge into the Pitt Street Mall. Here, the modern **Skygarden** is another money trap in the guise of an architectural delight. There is a wide range of men's and women's fashion shops within this six-storey masonry mannequin opened in 1990 (see *Shopping*). The building is crowned by a fine food court (though it's rather hard to find a seat at lunchtime), restaurant and bar area known as **Skydining.**

Sydney Tower, a.k.a. The Big Kebab

A must-visit is the Observation Deck at the **Sydney Tower** (open daily 9.30am–9.30pm except Saturday 9.30am–11pm, tel: 92297444). Take in the whole panoramic vista of Sydney from this vantage point 305m (1,000ft) high. Entry is from the podium level of the **Centrepoint** shopping centre (corner of Market, Pitt and Castlereagh streets). Take the lift all the way to the top.

The view is eye-boggling, especially through the powerful binoculars (look down into Government House). You may linger as long as you wish and there is plenty of information on what you are looking at. The **Sky Lounge** on the level below offers refreshments, while the two

revolving restaurants – one *à la carte*, the other self-service – have meals that are, well, surpassed by the views.

Oxford Street links the Central Business District to the eastern suburbs. Take a taxi there from wherever you are, while thinking about dinner. **Whitlam Square** (corner of Liverpool, Oxford, College and Wentworth streets) to **Taylor Square** (corner of Oxford, Bourke and Flinders streets) and beyond, up to Paddington, Oxford Street, is chock-a-block with economical geo-culinary eateries – **Raquel's Spanish Tavern** (No 98), **The Balkan** (No 209) and the **Angkor Wat Cambodia Restaurant** (No 227), plus a score more.

For thirsts and scenes there are fashion bars like the **Burdekin Hotel** (at Whitlam Square) and gay pubs like **The Exchange** (No 34) and, just past Taylor Square, the **Albury** (No 6). Opposite the Albury is the **Academy Twin Cinema**, which screens quality flicks.

Further up Oxford Street is **Paddington.** More eateries abound in this area, from **Sloane Rangers Cafe** (No 312) to the **Paddington Inn** bistro (No 388). Oxford Street, from the Town Hall onwards, is the diner's version of a stretch limo; the restaurant possibilities seem endless.

Kings Cross ('The Cross') is not to everyone's taste. **Darling-hurst Road** (between William and Macleay streets) is a gaping flesh wound of sex clubs, junk food, hookers and lookers, and 'there-but-for-the-grace-of-god-etc-etc' losers. Do *not* point your camera at most of the aforementioned,

Observation deck, Sydney Tower

lest both camera and you be trashed. **Pink Pussycat** (No 38A), **Love Machine** (No 60) and, across the street, **Porky's** are for ad libidinal floorshows. Pavement hustlers will give you full details of price and promised spectacle. A gamut of unmistakable sex shops offer the usual magazines and all that peculiar plumbing that is sold as 'marital aids', mostly to unmarried men.

Barons Pub (upstairs, 5 Roslyn Street), with its old sofas, back-gammon boards and winter fire is a welcome retreat from all this psychic tackiness, as is the **Round Midnight** jazz club opposite. A full frontal dance assault can be had at the **Hard Rock Cafe** (121 Crown Street) or **Studebakers** (19 Bayswater Road), or, if you're feeling a bit older, at the **Bourbon 'n' Beefsteak** (24 Darlinghurst Road) or its various neighbours. The **Soho Bar** (171 Victoria Street) is a trendy place to drink, while the next-door club, **The**

Sight, poses as hyper hip (reminding the great uncool majority of the great divide between yup and hip).

The **Landmark** in Macleay Street has a variety of dining, drinking and shopping opportunities. In Bayswater Road, **Bayswater Brasserie** (No 32) and the **Mesclun Brasserie** (opposite) provide elegant suppers. Bayswater's offshoot, Kellett Street, has a row of casual eateries of good repute (**Deans**, **Cafe Roma**, **Cafe Iguana**, **ZanziBar**, **Lemongrass**) co-existing in fine old terrace houses with neighbouring institutions of more dubious repute.

Finish this long day with quality coffee at **Cafe Hernandez** (60 Kings Cross Road) or, along the Darlinghurst side of Victoria Street (away from Kings Cross), at **Andiamo**, **Morgans** or **Nicolinas** – or try to catch someone's fancy at the **Cauldron** club (207 Darlinghurst Street).

Kings Cross promises a wickedly good time

Parks and Beaches

These itineraries are made for walking – through green leafy parks, past bits of history (with pit stops for coffee and cake), along heroic coasts, and, finally, to a good meal by the sea. (Note: no obligatory shopping for that opal-inlaid boomerang or duty-free lambskin designer T-shirt today.)

Kick off the day with a brief stroll through **Hyde Park**. Although not as magnificent as its London namesake, the park is worth a 10-minute stroll down its leafy central aisle which runs from Queens Square at the corner of Macquarie Street and St James Road, past the classical bronze figures of the Archibald Fountain, across Park Street, past Captain Cook (for whom the pigeons show scant respect) and on to the ANZAC **War Memorial** (open daily 10am–4pm, tel: 92677668). The 1934 art deco War Memorial (to Australians who served in the Boer War, World Wars I and II, and Korea, Malaya and Vietnam) features a dramatic sculpture of a dying soldier. From adjacent Liverpool or Elizabeth streets you can catch a taxi to Centennial Park.

Centennial Park – the green lungs of eastern Sydney – is most conveniently visited by car, but exploring by foot or rented bicycle is also fun. The park starts at the top end of Oxford Street, Paddington, and has a number of entrances. The one in York

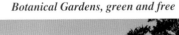

Botanical Gardens, green and free

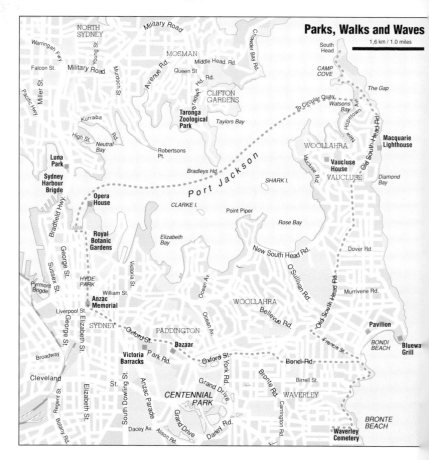

Road, Bondi Junction, provides the closest entrance to the city. Over 200 rolling hectares of lawns, trees, bridle paths, duck ponds and tranquillity await you. Created in 1888 to mark Australia's first centenary, the park has a restaurant (which serves breakfast, lunch, and morning and afternoon tea), a 1988 Bicentenary pavilion, and horse and bike hire facilities. Good for morning or afternoon runs or walks. Closes at sunset.

At this point – approaching snack time – you have a choice: either backtrack to Paddington (where you can also shop) or press on to Bondi Beach (where you generally don't). **Paddington**, if you're there on a Saturday, features a very good (if very 1960s) **bazaar** in the grounds of the Uniting Church at Oxford Street. Ex-

Paddington bookshop

pect craftware, clothing, jewellery, massages, gifts and snacks – a complete 'New Age meets Jimi Hendrix' experience – all at bargain prices. The rest of the street is a smorgasbord of boutiques, eateries and pubs. Recommended are the **New Editions Bookshop** and **Tea Rooms**

(328 Oxford Street) or the **Paddington Inn** (No 388). If you can spare the time, explore a few narrow side streets and their Victorian terrace houses. And if you happen to be here on a Tuesday, drop into the Army's **Victoria Barracks** (the imposing sandstone wall in Oxford Street surrounds it) for the not-to-be-missed, Changing-of-the-Guard ceremony at 10am.

A cool welcome

Bondi Beach is about a 10-minute drive further along Oxford Street and then Bondi Road. Bring your swimsuit and jump in – the water's fine between September and May, and almost bearable for a quick winter plunge. In summer, keep an eye on your clothes and valuables when you go swimming – petty theft is not unknown.

Bondi is Australia's most famous beach, a crescent kilometre of surf, sand and exertions. Located at both ends of the beach are safe rock pools and in the middle, an ornate old pavilion. The south end pool features the 'Bondi Icebergs' (ancient human walruses who swim year round), radical skateboard ramps and an array of near-naked sunbathers.

Bondi is also home to a huge range of eating establishments. In **Campbell Parade**, fronting the beach, try the **Lamrock Cafe** (No 72), the **Gelato Bar** (No 140), the **Swiss Grand Hotel** or the superbly sited first-floor cafe at **Ravesi's Corner** (corner of Hall Street) for coffee or lunch.

Sufficiently fuelled up, you can now stroll the easy, shore-hugging trail which heads south for a kilometre or so, from the Icebergs Pool around a surreal coastline of rocky coves and creamy surf to the 'glamarama' of **Tamarama Beach**. Keep going to the next beach, **Bronte**, and, if you still have the legs for it, up to Waverley's picturesque old **cliff-top cemetery**. Here, the dead have tombs with spectacular views of the coastline.

Take a taxi through the well-endowed Eastern Suburbs to the harbour's southern headland, **South Head**, near Watson's Bay. There's a good pub (for sinking a beer or two to the sinking sun) and also several seafood restaurants, the most famous of which is **Doyle's**. But first, walk south

Waverly Cemetery – tombs with a view

(away from the harbour entrance) along the ocean cliff, passing a spectacular drop called **The Gap** (once Sydney's favourite suicide spot), then on to the **Macquarie Lighthouse,** which has been in operation since 1790.

Drive back along Old South Head Road, drop down to the harbour, then out towards the tip of the peninsula to **Camp Cove.** Most of South Head is a naval base, but further around the shore (access by foot only) from Camp Cove, you can soak up rays and, if you wish, attention, at the nude **Lady Jane Beach** – a scene best described as 'voyeurs watching exhibitionists'. If private bathing is your scene, stay away, but it's quite a sideshow for people watchers. The elegant 1803 **Vaucluse House** (Tuesday to Sunday 10am–4.30pm, tel: 913371957) at Wentworth Road was the home of W C Wentworth, a colonial statesman and explorer. See what life was like in the 1800s and then have the delicious Devonshire cream tea served here.

There is a convenient ferry from Watson's Bay to Circular Quay. The last ferry departs **Watson's Bay Wharf** at 6.10pm on weekends and 2.47pm on weekdays. If you are not here in a car, extract yourself from the pub, the historic ambles, the overpriced fish 'n' chip menus and hop on board for the scenic ride.

In 40 minutes you're back in the city, having scanned the most expensive domestic real estate in the hemisphere. As Rose Bay and Double Bay ('Double Pay') roll away, there is a close-up of the Sydney Opera House – and you're back again in **Sydney Cove.**

For elegant dining, try the **Rockpool** (109 George Street North) or **Bilson's** (upper level, International Terminal), the **Imperial Peking Harbourside** (115 Circular Quay West) or **Merrony's** (Quay Apartments, 2 Albert Street), none of which will let you down – unless of course you haven't booked in advance.

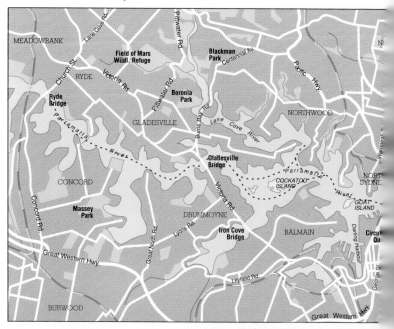

DAY 3

Sydney Harbour Cruises

Today's tour begins and ends at Circular Quay, and provides a good cross-section of everything that visitors and locals alike enjoy about the city of Sydney: Taronga Zoo, Manly, with its picturesque wharf and good restaurants, historic Fort Denison, shopping, and just cruising around Sydney harbour.

MANLY

Middle

Harbour

Spit Rd.

Sydney Harbour Nat'l Park

Grotto Pt.

...ary Rd.

Bradleys Head Rd.

MOSMAN

Sydney Harbour Nat'l Park

Middle Head

Fairfax Lookout

North Head

Sydney Harbour Nat'l Park

South Head

Taronga Zoo ■

Jackson

WATSONS BAY

The Gap

Pacific

Ocean

EMORNE POINT

Sydney Harbour Nat'l Park

Vaucluse House ■

Hopetoun Av.

■ Macquarie Lighthouse

Port

VAUCLUSE

CLARKE ISLAND

New South Head Rd.

DOUBLE BAY

South Head Rd.

Old South Head Rd.

Military Rd.

- - - 1 Manly Ferry
2 Meadowbank Ferries
- - - 3 Watsons Bay Ferries

Harbour Circuit

2,4 km / 1.5 miles

Many visitors to Sydney soon decide that Australians must be geometrically dyslexic: the tower of Australia Square is round and Circular Quay is rectangular. We can plead historical mischance that Circular Quay has corners. It was named 'Semi-circular Quay' in 1844 after landfill had been added to form a semi-circular shape. Subse-

Sunday juggler at Manly Corso

quent filling squared it off. Now known simply as 'The Quay', it is the main departure point for the network of ferry routes around Sydney Harbour. Information on State Transit ferries can be obtained at tel: 98189666.

A prime tour that takes you right along the main harbour is a ferry trip to **Manly**. There are two types of ferries to Manly. The traditional and cheaper ride takes 33 minutes one way. The newer,

Harbour ferry

faster and more expensive option, the Jet Cat, takes a mere 15 minutes to get to Manly.

Allow some time to explore Manly. **Manly Wharf** has been somewhat 'over-restored' to approximate the grandeur of the 1940s when it first opened. The adjoining harbour beach has also been upgraded, a few of its once numerous Norfolk Island pines nurtured back to health and some 90 shops and amusement park rides shoehorned onto the wharf. Like much of Manly, the area has a pleasant fun-in-the-sun sort of tackiness. A nearby attraction is the **Manly Oceanworld** (open daily 10am–5.30pm, tel: 99492644) on West Esplanade. Gaze up close at fish and other ocean creatures swimming in a giant aquarium as you travel on a moving walkway through a transparent underwater tunnel.

While in Manly, walk down the **Corso** pedestrian plaza, which runs a couple of hundred metres to the long expanse of ocean beach with its surfboard riders and lifesavers. Started by developer Henry Gordon Smith, the Corso was envisaged along the lines of England's Brighton beach. It was Smith who started ferry services to Manly in 1854, some 60 years before Bondi became popular. His house was near the stone kangaroo which still stands in Manly.

Most of the Corso is now a pedestrian mall. This is a good place to have lunch, and the choice of restaurants is endless. However, quality and prices are not closely related. For seafood, the **Rimini Fish Cafe** (35 South Steyne, tel: 99773880) is reasonable for both the quality of its seafood and its prices. **The Bower Restaurant** (7 Marine Parade, tel: 99775451) at Fairy Bower is another fair restaurant on a fine day. For an even more picturesque location, head for **Le Kiosk** (tel: 99774122), at the

Taronga Zoo overlooks the harbour

Koala at Taronga Zoo

edge of the sand on tiny Shelley Beach; the food is quite good and the setting is superb.

The network of inner city ferries (all departing from Circular Quay) stretches from Taronga Zoo to Darling Harbour and beyond to Birkenhead Point. A surprisingly pretty trip is the Rivercat ferry ride up to Meadowbank, far up the Parramatta River.

Taronga Zoo (open daily 9am–5pm, tel: 99692777; access by ferry from Jetty No 2, Circular Quay) definitely has one of the best settings of any zoo in the

Drinking in the scenery

world. Perched on a slope overlooking the harbour, it is scenically magnificent. The zoo houses wildlife from all around the world but is primarily the showcase for Australian fauna. All the indigenous animals of Australia – kangaroos, wallabies, koalas and the bizarre platypus and echidna – are on display, as well as a wide range of birds, fish and reptiles.

There are regular tours out to **Fort Denison** (Hegarty's Ferries, Jetty No 6, Circular Quay, tel: 92061167). The boats leave at noon from Monday to Friday, and at 10am, noon and 2pm on Saturday and Sunday. Remember to book in advance as only 50 people are allowed on each tour. Historically known as Pinchgut, a name that harkens back to the time the fort was used as a bread-and-water solitary confinement station for prisoners in the early days of the colony, the fort is perched on a rocky outcrop in the harbour near the Opera House. Bedecked with fortifications which look like a stage setting for a comic opera, this tiny fort was originally part of Sydney's defence against a feared Russian invasion during the Crimean War (1855–1857). The rocky islet was levelled by convict labour in the 1830s and the rubble used as land fill at Circular Quay. The fort – named after the Governor of the day – and its tower are well worth visiting and the views of the Sydney skyline are simply spectacular.

There several interesting harbour cruise options if you have the time. To cover the main points of Sydney Harbour, try the **Main Harbour Cruise** (Jetty No 4, Circular Quay, tel: 92564670) which operates daily. The vessel departs Circular Quay every 2 hours between 9.30am and 3.30pm, calling at The Rocks, the Opera House, Watsons Bay, Taronga Zoo and Darling Harbour. A useful feature of this cruise is that you can disembark and reboard when and where you like throughout the day.

Captain Cook Cruises (tel: 92061111) runs some 14 harbour cruises each day. Probably the most popular of all is the Coffee Cruise that departs daily at 10am and 2.15pm. It's a 2½-hour voyage (with useful commentary) onboard the company's most modern vessel along the main harbour and past the waterfront mansions of Middle Harbour. Put your feet up and take in the sights as coffee or tea is served to passengers.

Circular Quay snack-time

PICK & MIX

1. Colonial Architecture

This tour is a horseshoe-shaped excursion from the Town Hall to Circular Quay and back to Hyde Park. Along the way much of Sydney's colonial heritage can be seen. The trip takes about an hour if you just look at the facades. However, if you plan to venture inside the places mentioned (and many are worth a closer look), you should allow a half-day or more.

Start this tour at Queens Square (corner of Macquarie Street and St James Road), near an exit from St James railway station. It is a fitting place to begin because here you'll find three marvellous colonial Georgian buildings designed by convict architect Francis Greenway. These are **Hyde Park Barracks** (now a museum dealing with the social history of New South Wales), the **NSW Supreme Court** and **St James' Church**. For a cheap and tasty breakfast, or lunch (depending on what time you started out on this tour) and an excellent overview of the city and the harbour, visit the cafeteria on the 14th level of the Law Courts opposite. It's okay, this is open to the public.

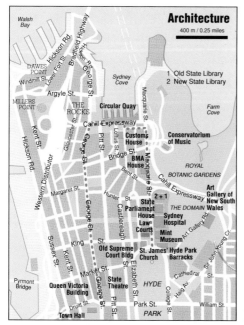

The **Mint Museum** (open daily 10am–5pm), with its Georgian facade, is the restored south wing of the old Rum Hospital, built in the 1840s and now the home of numismatic and philatelic displays. It was called the Rum Hospital because the first hospital that was built in 1816 had

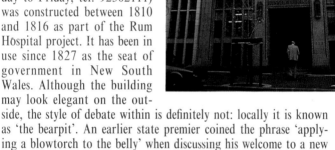

BMA House, Macquarie Square

been paid for by the money obtained from granting the building contractors a lucrative monopoly on the import of rum into the colony.

The enormous sandstone complex next door is **Sydney Hospital**, built in 1894 with some input from Florence Nightingale. Walk around the side of the building into the rear courtyard and check out the beautiful gingerbread brick **Nightingale Building** and the antique fountain. The **State Parliament House** (open for inspection 9am to 4.30pm Monday to Friday, tel: 92302111) was constructed between 1810 and 1816 as part of the Rum Hospital project. It has been in use since 1827 as the seat of government in New South Wales. Although the building may look elegant on the outside, the style of debate within is definitely not: locally it is known as 'the bearpit'. An earlier state premier coined the phrase 'applying a blowtorch to the belly' when discussing his welcome to a new leader of the opposition.

Towards the southern end of Macquarie Street is the **new State Library** (Monday to Saturday 9am–9pm, Sunday 2–6pm). Opened in 1988, it's a pleasant place to visit, with endless reading material, public areas and a good cafe. The library is joined by an enclosed overhead pedestrian bridge to the **old State Library** (tel: 92301414), housed in one of the most impressive buildings in Sydney. It is commonly referred to as the Mitchell Library, although this is the name of just one wing of this vast storehouse of books. The main reading room is an airy hall, naturally lit by an imposing skylight.

Across the road at 135-137 Macquarie Street stands a prime representative of Sydney's art deco buildings: the BMA (British Medical Association) **House**, built in 1930. The elaborate facade of this building is truly wonderful and well worth a close inspection. Note the fine details like its stone koalas.

As you walk down Macquarie

The Conservatorium of Music

Street towards the Opera House and the harbour, you will pass the the **Royal Botanical Gardens** on your right. This swathe of greenery with its duck ponds, Victorian statues and hidden groves provides a pleasant break from the concrete and traffic of the city. The white castellated structure in Macquarie Street, right at the city entrance to the Cahill Expressway, is the **Conservatorium of Music** (tel: 92301222). This unusual building is open to the public; concerts take place here regularly. The 'Con', as it is otherwise known, looks far too elaborate for its present purpose – it is even more incongruous to think that it was originally built as the stables for the nearby Government House.

The **Art Gallery of New South Wales** (Monday to Saturday 10am–5pm, Sunday noon–5pm, tel: 92251700) is a short walk across the park behind the Parliament House, known as the Domain. Its imposing Victorian facade and serried statues in alcoves were added to the original 1885 structure at the time of Federation. The gallery houses a strong collection of Australian works and a weaker one of dark and foreboding European paintings. There are usually special exhibitions on – always popular with Sydneysiders. Check the Saturday *Sydney Morning Herald* for details. The Art Gallery Restaurant (open for lunch only, tel: 92325425) is very good and relatively inexpensive but the wait for a table can be long.

Return to Macquarie Street and turn left into Albert Street, along a short steep hill to Circular Quay. Sadly, the only surviving historic building along the Quay is the **Customs House**, between Young and Loftus streets. It is located where the Union Jack was reputedly flown for the first time in Sydney Cove. For passersby, the most notable feature of this 1885 building is the intricately carved stone coat-of-arms over the entrance and the decidedly unamused visage of Queen Victoria above the door.

Across Alfred Street and under the remarkably ugly Cahill Expressway and Circular Quay railway station stands **Circular**

Sydney Town Hall

Quay. The Cahill Expressway, named after a New South Wales premier, seemed like a great step forward in transport when it was built in 1958. Now, it is rightly seen as an eyesore that cuts the city off from the harbour. To the western (or Harbour Bridge) side of the Quay is the classic but monolithic Art Deco building of the **Museum of Contemporary Art** (open daily 11am–6pm).

Upon reaching George Street, skip **The Rocks** (the area up to your right) at this time and walk left up George Street a few blocks past Wynyard Station to Market Street. The **State Theatre** (49 Market Street, tel: 92642431) between George and Pitt streets is an astonishingly ornate picture palace built in 1929. Even if the film being played inside is not your cup of tea, the statues, chandeliers and marble staircase inside this flamboyant gilded structure will leave an indelible impression on you.

Returning to George Street, cross the road and enter the vast **Queen Victoria Building** (QVB) that occupies a complete city block. For years, the QVB was an ugly blot on the cityscape: a few shops

QVB facade, George Street

clung to a tenuous existence at street level and the dingy interior housed the Sydney City Library. It was closed for several years, then in 1986 it emerged, chrysalis-like, from the renovator's scaffolding, irradiated by the A$75 million allegedly spent on it. Both the shops and structure of the QVB compete for your attention. The basement 'Eats Street' has an array of food outlets.

A good finishing point for this tour is the **Town Hall**, on the corner of George and Park streets, with its startling mixture of styles reflecting the fact that several architects had worked on the original building before it opened in 1889 and on its extensions. Irrespective of aesthetics, the Town Hall is an imposing building and its steps are a favourite meeting place for Sydneysiders. Inside is a fascinating blend of marble and crystal chandeliers; plus the very impressive, but sadly underutilised, six-keyboard, 8,500-pipe grand organ (recently restored) – and truly terrible acoustics, a fact long rued by Town Hall concert-goers.

2. The Sydney Opera House

Whether it's to see a show, have dinner, take a guided tour or merely walk around it, every visitor to Sydney should look over the Opera House. Despite the somewhat unfinished look inside the shell, it is a remarkable structure in a spectacular setting.

It is important to bear in mind that the Sydney Opera House is a public building. In a way, its world-famous profile is only a sec-

Architectural Amblings

Visitors with time to venture further afield should include Elizabeth Bay House and, at Parramatta, the governor's country residence and Elizabeth Farm House in their itineraries. **Elizabeth Bay House** at 7 Onslow Avenue, Elizabeth Bay (Tuesday to Sunday 10am–4.30pm, tel: 93582344) is a superb 1835 Regency mansion with a stunning interior and great views of the harbour.

Parramatta, the second settlement established in the colony, is home to many historic buildings. **Old Government House** (tel: 96358149), built in 1790 and extended by governors Hunter and Macquarie in the following 26 years, is now a museum containing 19th-century Australian furniture. Located in Parramatta Park, the house was the official vice-regal country residence of the period and is the country's oldest public building. **Elizabeth Farm House** at 70 Alice Street (Tuesday to Sunday 10am–4.30pm, tel: 96359488), commenced in 1793 and contains parts of Australia's oldest surviving European building, having been the residence of merino sheep farmers, John and Elizabeth Macarthur. Macarthur dominated colonial society and his house was an important social centre for the colony. Today, it has been turned into a museum furnished in early colonial style.

ondary aspect: this is no mere monument to be viewed from afar. Rather, you are welcome to attend performances at any of its theatres: the Opera Theatre (which seats 1,500), the Concert Hall (2,700), the Drama Theatre (550) and various other halls accommodating between 150 and 420 people. Or, you can dine in one of several restaurants, drink at one of the bars, or merely walk around and inside the building and admire the vision of its designer. You won't be alone – about half of all visitors to Australia visit the sail-like structure on Bennelong Point.

The Opera House looks so right in its setting that it is difficult to remember that it replaced a dilapidated set of tram sheds incongruously located on a piece of prime real estate at the eastern end of Circular Quay. Its truly amazing when you realise that the creator of the structure conceived the striking design after only seeing photographs of the site.

In 1957, the New South Wales government conducted a worldwide competition for the design of an opera house. Some 220 entries were received but one, by 38-year-old Danish architect Jørn Utzon, stood out. Art critic Robert Hughes described that original design as little more than 'a magnificent doodle' but the white sails soaring above the harbour were a vision which showed genius in more than spectacle alone. Columnless performance spaces, stage mechanisms located vertically above and below the proscenium, and the promise of perfect acoustics all accommodated in a building of functional and aesthetic virtuosity, combined to convince the international judging panel.

Utzon and his team began to translate the schematic vision into concrete and steel in 1959 with a projected completion date of 1963. However, construction was slow, the political backbiting was intense, and the price rose more quickly than its 67-m (220-ft) high sails. Even though the building was paid for by state-run lotteries, Utzon was ordered to reduce the ever-growing budget by working with a team of government architects. He refused to compromise and in 1966 quit the project and Australia in a huff. 'Tear it down' was his parting shot – he has never seen the completed building.

The dramatic Sydney Opera House

Bennelong Restaurant, Opera House

Utzon would have had to wait a while to do so anyhow. The flawed masterpiece was opened on 20 October 1973 by Queen Elizabeth in one of those grand harbourside occasions that Sydney does so well. The major performance on that opening night was of Beethoven's Ninth Symphony. The final reckoning revealed that the building had cost A$102 million and taken 16 years to complete: a far cry from the original estimates of A$7 million and four years.

Today, with all the acrimony in the past, Sydney is justifiably proud of the Opera House. Its statistics remain awesome. The roof weighs 158,000 tons and is supported by 350km (217 miles) of cables. The one million anti-fungal roof tiles never need cleaning. Over 6,200sq m (67,000sq ft) of tinted French glass enclose its 'Space Gothic' interiors. The Concert Hall organ, with 10,500 pipes, is the largest mechanical-action organ in the world. The whole complex covers 1.8ha (4½ acres). And, as Utzon intended, the acoustics in the Opera Theatre are regarded as 'perfect' (although the orchestra pit is too small for many purposes).

To select a performance to attend at the Opera House, consult the entertainment sections of the daily newspapers or call the Opera House box office at tel: 92507777. The Opera House is not the exclusive domain of those who can afford the top-priced opera tickets. There is something for everyone. Within its spectacular shell is a varied offering of drama, cinema, dance, orchestral recitals, rock concerts, conferences, exhibitions, outdoor concerts and more. There is considerable variety every day and it attracts over 1.6 million spectators each year.

A tempting event for the visitor is the 'Tour, Dinner, Performance' package which includes what it says, with the performance being either opera, ballet, theatre or music. Accordingly,

Forecourt restaurant, Opera House

prices can range from A$111 to A$211. Book through the Opera House's Tourism Services Department at tel: 91250783.

If you rather not watch a performance, organized tours run every day between 9am and 4pm. To check tour availability you should call tel: 92507250.

There are three restaurants at the Opera House. The most informal is the **Concourse**, which serves upmarket sandwiches, light meals and great desserts along with a wide selection of wines and cocktails. At the very tip of Bennelong Point, the **Harbour Restaurant** (tel: 92507191), like the Concourse, is best experienced sitting outside on a summer afternoon. It is the complex's mid-priced restaurant offering reasonable value for money and scenic splendour. High dining at the Opera House is in the **Bennelong** restaurant (tel: 92507578) within its own sail-capped building; the hand that guides it is famed Sydney restaurateur Gay Bilson. Meals are quite expensive but the standard of service and food is very good. In this sublime setting, your pleasure of the food and view is also enhanced by knowing that it is not every day that you dine inside a national symbol.

3. Museums and Art Galleries

Lay Sydney's museums and art galleries end to end and they would stretch further than a visitor's attention span. The following are but a few of the closest and the most interesting from which to chose for one morning of acculturation saturation.

Observatory Hill, in The Rocks area, is an appropriate starting point for a Sydney culture cruise. The city's highest natural point, with a spectacular view of Port Jackson, it was the original site of a windmill (1796), then a half-built fort (1803) and finally, in 1848, a shipping signal station. The signal station survives as the **Sydney Observatory** but its era for studying the little-known southern sky has passed; city pollution now making serious astronomical study near impossible. Today, it is the **Museum of Astronomy** (Monday to Friday 2–5pm, Saturday and Sunday 10am–5pm, tel: 92412478). Most evenings the museum conducts night-sky observation sessions for lay skywatchers.

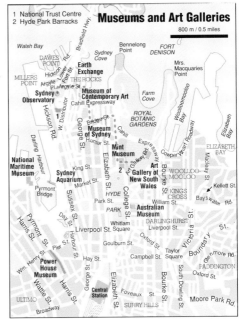

On the same hill above The Rocks, Governor Macquarie built a military hospital in 1815. It is now the **National Trust Centre**, and includes the **S H Ervin Gallery** (Tuesday to Friday 11am–5pm, Saturday and Sunday noon–5pm, tel: 92580174), one of the largest non-commercial galleries in Sydney and specialising in the very best of Australian figurative art.

Also at The Rocks, at 18 Hickson Road, the revolutionary geological and mining museum **Earth Exchange** (open daily 10am–5pm, tel: 92512422) is an interactive, audio-visual trip through the Earth's mineral and fossil history, with an emphasis on Australian minerals, plus a simulated underground mine. The Earth Exchange features Australia's best mineral collection, a simulation of a Sydney earthquake and Australia's largest gold nugget. The gift shop stocks a wide variety of gemstones (including opals), minerals and related books.

Holdsworth Gallery, Paddington

For contemporary art that is thought-provoking and ever fresh, visit the **Museum of Contemporary Art** at 132 George Street (open daily 11am–6pm, tel: 92524033) in the Circular Quay area. The museum features changing exhibitions of Australian and international contemporary art works, housed in a 1940s art deco building.

Just up the hill from Circular Quay, at the corner of Bridge and Phillip streets, opposite Hotel Inter-Continental, is the terrific, new **Museum of Sydney** (open daily 10am–5pm, tel: 92515988). Occupying the site of the first Government House, the museum showcases the history of Sydney, from the time of Aborigines to the present. Don't miss the forecourt pole sculptures.

A short walk away on Macquarie Street is the **Mint Museum** (open daily 10am–5pm, tel: 92170333), a painstakingly restored wing of the 1816 'Rum Hospital'. In the early days of the colony, the economy literally floated on rum, the de facto currency. Governor William Bligh – of *Bounty* fame – experienced yet another rebellion when he attempted to mop up these 'liquid assets'. The two-storeyed building housed surgeons before it became, in 1851, the first branch of the Royal Mint outside London, producing gold coins until 1927. Today, the museum specialises in Australian gold.

The neighbouring Georgian-style **Hyde Park Barracks** (open daily 10am–5pm, except Tuesday noon–5pm, tel: 92170333) was commissioned by Governor Macquarie in 1819 and designed by convict architect Francis Greenway to provide accommodation for

Decorated Aboriginal wood-winds

convicts. Later, the building was used as a lodging house for single women and orphaned girls. In 1979, it was converted into a museum documenting the social history of New South Wales, from the early convict days to the 1950s, with displays on the themes of immigration, public celebrations and the founding of Australia.

A short walk across the Domain parkland from Macquarie Street brings you to the **Art Gallery of New South Wales** (Monday to Saturday 10am–5pm, Sunday noon–5pm, tel: 92251700) in Art Gallery Road. Its classical facade belies the flexibility and breadth of the Australian, international and Asian collections within. Be sure to see the specimens of Aboriginal and Papua New Guinean tribal art. If you haven't had a surfeit of museums by now, continue to the **Australian Museum** (Tuesday to Saturday, 10am–5pm, Sunday and Monday noon–5pm, tel: 93398111), at the corner of William and College streets. This museum holds the country's largest collection of natural history exhibits, with well-displayed marine life, bird and mammal sections, and an excellent Aboriginal Australia display.

Back across town, just west of Darling Harbour, at 500 Harris Street, is the superstar of Sydney museums, the hugely popular **Power House Museum** (open daily 10am–5pm, tel: 92170111). This 1899 power station and former tram depot has been renovated to

New South Wales Art Gallery

house the huge collection of of material the Museum of Applied Arts and Sciences has been accumulating since the 1880s. Visitor participation is encouraged in the many 'hands-on' displays. Displays such as the state's first train engine, bush kitchens, crafts and fashion, planes and even a space shuttle are grouped around four major themes – science and technology, decorative arts, and social history. Allow plenty of time for the Powerhouse – kids love it and it loves them.

Darling Harbour has two nautical museums, both on the western shore. Beneath the sail-like roofs of the **National Maritime Museum** (open daily 10am–5pm) is an exciting re-creation of Australia's long maritime history.

These are numerous commercial art galleries catering to different tastes, from outback kitsch to postmodern obsessive. Check the *Sydney Morning Herald* listings ('Metro' section) on Friday or Saturday for details, or see the *Yellow Pages*. Many private galleries are to be found in the Paddington-Woollahra area. For contemporary Australian paintings, sculptures and installation art, check out the **Robin Gibson**, **Mori** and **Ivan Dougherty** galleries. Take a look also at the Brett Whitelay Studio (Saturday and Sunday 10am–4pm, tel: 92251744) where the works of the late, mercurial Australian painter are displayed. For Aboriginal art, the best is to be found at the **Art Gallery of New South Wales** and the **Australian Museum**.

4. The Spit to Manly Harbour Walk

An easy, 8-km (5-mile) trail leads around the northern foreshores of Sydney Harbour from Spit Bridge to Manly Wharf. In places, this unparalleled eyeful of Australian bush and bay is much as Captain Arthur Phillip would have seen it back in 1787.

Grab a sunny day and a pair of light walking shoes, a sunhat and water bottle, and head out for 3 hours of coastal foot cruising. 'The Spit' – that is 'sandspit' – is located about 30 minutes north of the city, via North Sydney, Neutral Bay, Mosman and Spit Junction. Government buses from York Street in the city will get you there, but it will be far quicker to catch a taxi.

After arriving at the northern end of the **Spit Bridge**, cross the road to the eastern side, descend to a grassy clearing, then follow the path east around the foreshore. Generally well marked, the trail becomes temporarily obscure in only one or two places – if so, just retrace your footsteps and look again.

Leaf-framed views of sandstone headlands, ultramarine-gone-ultraviolet views of harbour expanse, sails and ferry wakes, bomboras (reef waves), buoys and picnic coves – all these will delight the

Right, Sydney Harbour shores

Manly Wharf

hiker. Bring your swimming gear and take a dip from time to time, although in summer you should be mindful of sharks. It has been a quarter of a century since the last fatal attack inside the harbour, but why risk becoming a footnote in history?

As you amble along (and there really is no rush), you will pass the front lawns of sumptuous houses, but as culture surrounds nature – and this seems odd – you will see almost no birds or fauna, and certainly no kangaroos or koalas. Nevertheless, nature at least will not shrink any further here, for much of the trail runs through sections of **Sydney Harbour National Park**. In parts, there is evidence of bushfires: these happen infrequently, and only in high summer – although in 1990 a Japanese tour group had the thrill of being rescued from a fire in this area by a helicopter evacuation. Along the way illustrated plaques inform you about nearby native flora, such as grevillea, figs, banksia, scentless rosewood, angophora, wandering jew and 'black boys', all of which are protected (so don't pick them).

The first section of the walk, 1½km (1 mile) to **Clontarf Beach**, takes about 40 minutes, skirting a shady bay before arriving at Clontarf, which has shark-proof swimming, picnic facilities and

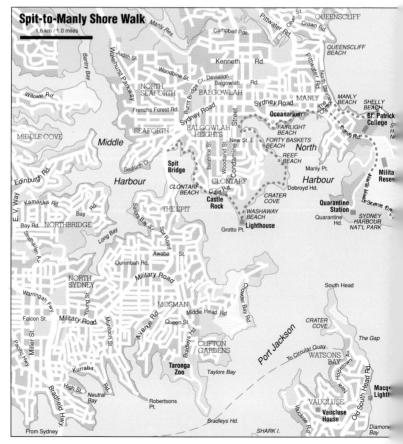

Spit-to-Manly Shore Walk

1.6 km / 1.0 miles

road access. It is possible to cover only portions of this walk, exiting where the trail meets a local road, such as at Beatty Street, Balgowlah – although here you'll be a long way from public transportation. Continue on to **Castle Rock** and **Grotto Point**, site of a pretty lighthouse that from afar looks like a tiny Greek island chapel. From close up, the lighthouse is far less interesting, but the point it sits upon gives a great view of what one of the 'First Fleeters' described as 'the finest harbour in the universe'. On a clear day you can see what he meant.

Middle Harbour

You soon approach the halfway point on the trek, about 3km (2 miles) and 85 minutes later. Nearby are Aboriginal carvings – made by a tribe that was wiped out by smallpox in the early days of the colony – which you may stumble upon if you are lucky. They are not signposted in order to avoid the grafitti of contemporary 'yobbo' tribesmen. Easier to spot is **Washaway Beach** below Grotto Point, a nudist beach and a good place for a swim. Next come **Crater Cove**, **Dobroyd Head** (spot the tiny rock huts in the cove – fishermen and drop-outs lived in them for years) and **Reef Beach**, the latter being another nudist beach. Anyone arriving at Reef Beach by boat should be aware of the dangerous swell: each year regulars keep score of the boats that come ashore capsized.

When you hit **Forty Baskets Beach**, the modest attire of the swimmers signals the end of the 'wild' part of the walk. From here on it's mainly a suburban stroll for the next 30 minutes around the foreshores of **Fairlight Beach**.

This potted view of the Australian bush now gives way to the leisure possibilities of Manly – named so because this is what Captain Phillip of the First Fleet thought of the local Aborigines (in fact, they were so bloody manly that they speared him!). The highlight of the **Manly Oceanworld** (open daily 10am–5.30pm, tel: 99492644) on West Esplanade is a moving footway which takes you through a transparent acrylic tunnel above which fish and sharks swim. Other attractions in Manly include the **Art Gallery** (also on West Esplanade), a newly polished-up ferry wharf (plus Ferris wheel, bars, restaurants and shops), a cinema, and of course the great harbour and ocean beaches.

After a refreshing ale, coffee or juice at **Manly Wharf**, if there's some kick left in your heels, head east on the **Corso**. This street

Manly Corso – buskers, beers and boardshorts

runs the few hundred metres from the harbour to the ocean beach, past a surfeit of take-away food joints, pseudo-Scandinavian ice-cream shops, pubs and some real hit-and-miss restaurants. (If re-heated crêpes served without apology are your idea of a hit then you won't want to miss some of these places.) Manly has many other eating options, from fish 'n' chips and Thai along the Corso, to surf-view fine dining at **Gilbert's** in the Manly Pacific Parkroyal Hotel.

And then you're at **South Steyne**, facing the great Pacific Ocean and the famous expanse of surf and sand which is **Manly Beach**. The once stately, now balding, Norfolk Island pines attest to the ravages of atmospheric pollution, detergents and salt. On Sundays, a market is held here on the esplanade, with the usual ceramic, leather and other bric-a-brac offerings.

Facing the sea, to your left – at the far end of the beach – is **Queenscliff**, and to your right the cove of **Shelly Beach**, the point and surf of **Fairy Bower**, and the **North Head** of Sydney Harbour. The Gothic-looking stone building on the hill is **St Patrick's College**. For more information about this lovely suburb, drop into

Bushwalking, harbour shore

the **Manly Visitors Information Bureau** (tel: 99771088) at South Steyne.

Keep walking south (to your right) along the esplanade to the South Steyne Surf Club, then around the ocean-side path, where after 5 minutes you will reach the **Bower Restaurant** (7 Marine Parade, tel: 99775451) for a well-earned lunch. The food is fresh and unpretentious. If you're in the mood for seafood, continue walking for another few minutes to Shelly Beach, where you will find an enclave of homes and a more expensive beachside restaurant, **Le Kiosk** (Marine Parade, tel: 99774122), preferably having booked beforehand.

Return to Manly by the same route, or if you have time, by taxi for a quick look at **North Head**, the gem of the Sydney Harbour National Park. **Fairfax Lookout** at the point provides a great view. Back towards Manly, on the harbour side, is the defunct 1833 **Quarantine Station**, which is now administered as a tourist attraction by the NSW National Parks and Wildlife Service.

After this very hectic morning, you have the option of returning to Circular Quay from Manly Wharf, either quickly by Jet Cat, or more placidly by ferry.

A lazy day at Manly Cove Beach

5. Sydney Harbour Bridge to North Sydney

The pedestrian walkway on the eastern side of the Sydney Harbour Bridge is perhaps Sydney's most underutilised free tourist attraction: the walk to the North Shore is memorable and puts the massive scale of the bridge into true proportion.

If you catch a train or ferry back from Milsons Point/Kirribilli, the return trip can take as little as 2 hours, but it is better to allocate more time. The best time to take this walk is at dawn as the sun is rising between Sydney Heads and turning the water in the harbour into a creamy liquid gold. The place to start this tour is **Dawes Point Park**, directly under the bridge in The Rocks. From here, you get a daunting worm's-eye view of the monumental structure overhead. Spare a thought for the architects and engineers who stood here in the 1920s and envisaged a span reaching across the deep harbour.

One of the largest arch bridges in the world, **Sydney Harbour Bridge** was built from both ends, starting in 1923 and joining in 1930 at a cost of just under 10 million pounds – the loan which financed it was finally paid off in 1988. The stone pylons are largely decorative and the arch is supported by four huge pins each 35cm (14in) in diameter and 4¼m (13½ft) long. The total weight of steel

in the bridge is 53,000 tonnes. It takes 10 years to paint the bridge and the task consumes over 30,000 litres (60,600 gallons) of paint (ask Paul Hogan; he used to be a rigger on the bridge).

To access the bridge's eastern walkway, walk to Cumberland Street at the top of the Argyle steps off Argyle Street. Bicycle riders will be glad to know that there is a cycleway on the western side of the bridge. Once on the walkway, your path is clear, as is your view, although only a short way along you'll notice that a block of flats intrudes upon your view of the harbour. This is subsidised housing provided by the government – and in turn providing some of the best residential views in Sydney. This building was a point of some contention among Sydneysiders. But then, nearly everything in Sydney is both political and controversial. It was under the shadow of political turmoil in the Great Depression that the Sydney Harbour Bridge opened in March 1932.

Just as the structure has become an enduring part of the city landscape, the opening ceremony has become an embarrassing part of Australian history. Before state Premier Jack Lang could ceremonially cut the ribbon to open the bridge, Captain de Groot of

the paramilitary New Guard rode up and slashed it with his sword, declaring the bridge open on behalf of 'the decent and loyal citizens of New South Wales'. The ribbon was eventually retied and the official ceremony continued. Nevertheless, the political frame could not be so easily reconstructed: within a couple of months, Lang had been dismissed from office by the governor and the far right of New South Wales politics had prevailed.

The southeastern pylon of the bridge is open to the public from Saturday to Tuesday between 10am and 5pm in winter and every day in summer. Inside is a historical display on the building of the bridge, and, at the top of a 200-step climb, a lookout with a wonderful panorama of Sydney.

Unfortunately, the top of the

North Sydney Olympic Swimming Pool

arch of the bridge is not open to the public, and hidden cameras have reduced the number of brave souls who climb it only to be arrested upon their descent.

North Sydney is the ever-growing centre for much of Sydney's media and advertising industry. These high-profile industries are well supported by several upmarket shopping centres and stylish restaurants. **Armstrongs Brasserie** (1–7 Napier Street, North Sydney, tel: 99552066) serves an array of multinational dishes often described as modern Australian cuisine. It's a good brasserie combining lively decor with imaginative cooking. Alternatively, the **Malaya**, in the old fire station at 86 Walker Street (tel: 99554306), is culturally purer, right down to the rather off-hand service. It has a pleasantly refreshing modern decor and there are some bland dishes on the menu, but if your system needs a chilli steam-clean, order a *laksa*. It looks like noodle soup but tastes like lava.

After a brisk stroll across the bridge (or an incendiary *laksa*), the perfect way to finish the day is to walk down to **North Sydney Olympic Swimming Pool,** almost under the northern end of the bridge. In summer, this is an excellent place to swim and sightsee simultaneously – especially if you swim backstroke. Watching the peak hour crowds stuck in heavy bridge traffic while you wallow languidly below is the icing on the cake.

Just to the west is **Luna Park** (Monday to Thursday 10am–8pm, Friday and Saturday 10am–11pm), a Sydney landmark for over 60 years that has just re-opened as a contemporary amusement park. The smiling face that forms the entrance is a variation on earlier ones and Coney Island has been restored with rides like a new Big Dipper, dodgem cars and a Rotor. Entry is free and you buy tickets for the attractions inside.

From the north shore you might like to catch a taxi back to the city via the the Sydney Harbour tunnel, which opened in August 1992. It may be a technological achievement, but as some Sydneysiders found out, it's not for claustrophobics.

6. A Pub Crawl

To get 'blotto' is not the point of this itinerary, although it may be an occupational hazard. Drink light beer or lemon squash to maintain the regimen. A tour of these watering holes gives you a glimpse of ordinary Australians and some of the social history woven into – or formulated in – Sydney's pubs.

This crawl can start anytime after mid-morning, about the time when most Sydney pubs open. Begin at Sydney's beginnings... at **The Rocks**. You have a choice of three historical establishments: the

Old-style beer delivery – The Rocks

Lord Nelson Hotel (corner of Kent and Argyle Streets), the oldest hotel in town, and now a bar, brasserie and brewery; the **Fortune of War Hotel** (137 George Street), which occupies the oldest hotel site in Sydney (it was built in 1922, replacing its 1839 namesake); and the **Hero of Waterloo** (81 Windmill Street), also a contender for the title of oldest pub. The Hero's cellars were reputedly used as holding cells for 'press-ganged' sailors back in the 'roaring days'. All around are the Victorian-era houses of Lower Fort Street and the great wooden wharf sheds of Walsh Bay's Hickson Road.

But first, a word on Sydney alcohol culture. The colony of New South Wales was founded on rum, and by 1808 (the time of Governor William Bligh of the *Bounty* fame), it was the quasi-official currency of the colony. Today, however, beer, 'the amber fluid', is Australia's favourite tipple – the country has even been called 'the Land of the Liquid Lunch' – and an entire vocabulary has revolved around the drink. 'Tinnies' are tin cans, 'twisties' are twist-top bottles, 'stubbies' are also bottles. Fosters, Tooheys, Coopers, Castlemaine XXXX (pronounced 'Four Ex' – reputedly because Queenslanders can't spell 'beer') and Swan are some of the major brands, followed by the so-called

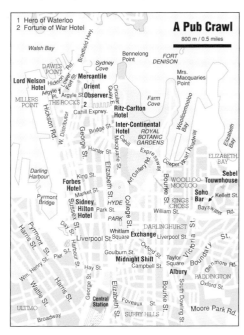

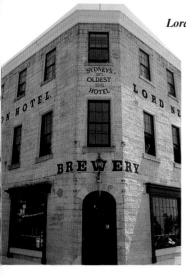

'boutique' beers like Hahn, Eumundi, Redback, Dogbolter etc.

Also available, but more expensive, are imports like Heineken, NZ Steinlager, Corona, Guinness and others. Australian beers are served very cold in pubs and are generally higher in alcohol content than standard British or American brews. The 'middy', which costs around A$2 and up, is a manageable-sized beer of about half a pint, but drinking the larger 'schooner', around A$3 and up, is not going to get you through today's agenda if you sink one at each stop.

For a change of 'neck oil', try Queensland's Bundaberg rum, commonly referred to as 'Bundy'. Australia also produces excellent wines, but these are not served by the glass over the counter, although they can be purchased by the bottle. 'House' wine by the glass will be the very *ordinaire* but passable 'Château Cardboard', ie, from a boxed cask behind the bar counter.

While Australian pub culture is unmistakably male, all pubs have mixed drinking – although in some, women may prefer not to tread. In all pubs mentioned herein, visitors – both male and female – should feel quite at ease.

Meanwhile, back in **George Street** at The Rocks... move into the post-convict era at either the Orient, Observer or Mercantile hotels. The re-gentrified **Orient** (corner of Argyle Street) is a familiar after-work meeting place for office workers and professionals and serves good food.

The more proletarian **Mercantile** has a distinctly Irish flavour and often features folk singers – and Guinness-fuelled riotous times on St Patrick's Day or Melbourne Cup Day. The **Observer** is equally welcoming and 'fair dinkum' Australian. In The Rocks' sea of ersatz Oz, the latter two places are sanctuaries for the sort of ordinary Australians for whom 'duty-free' means nothing more than a day off work and who wouldn't be caught dead at the 'barby' in a Ken Done apron.

Up in **Macquarie Street** there are two hotels (you'd never call them 'pubs') which architecturally symbolise the Sydney of the late 20th century – by glueing it onto 19th-century buildings. Both are five-star international chain hotels, featuring the nostalgia and elegant schizophrenia of architectural 'facade-ism'.

The **Ritz-Carlton** (No 93) has sprung, miraculously cured, out of the bricks of a former VD clinic and hospital, while the much larger **Inter-Continental** (No 117) sprouts from the shell of the once lovely sandstone Colonial Treasury Building. In the former establishment, sink something like a stout or port in the clubby instant antiquity of **The Bar.** In the latter, tea in the central courtyard is quite genteel, but even ordinary whisky in the lounge bar on level

34 is breathtaking. The view stretches from the Sydney Domain, through the Harbour Heads and almost to New Zealand. The prices too are elevated, but with a vista like this it's a bargain high.

Back down to earth, the **Forbes Hotel** at the corner of York and King streets is another piece of renovated history, but without the high-rise implant. Lots of polished wood, brass and stained glass in this colonial Central Business District boozer and eatery. Today, it's a yuppie hangout and a good place to rub shoulders with the after-office crowd.

A 5-minute walk away in George Street (opposite the Queen Victoria Building), in the bowels of the **Sydney Hilton Hotel**, is the extraordinary **Marble Bar**. So precious a creation is this 1893 darling that it was dismantled, then reassembled stone by stone when its original home, the George Adams Hotel, was removed in the early 1970s to make way for the Hilton. It is all green marble chintz, original paintings, stained glass and ornate columns – and an indicator of the great wealth which poured through Sydney in the last century. Lots of jazz and rock played here.

Doorman, Ritz-Carlton

As night closes in you can check out the gay pubs in **Oxford Street**, notably **The Exchange** (No 34), **Midnight Shift** (No 85) and in Paddington the **Albury** (No 6). They're flamboyant (and 'glamboyant'), and have raucous, camped-up entertainment. In Kings Cross, the **Celebrities Bar** in the **Sebel Townhouse** (23 Elizabeth Bay Road) is intimate, fairly hetero, and you might even catch sight of the stars and entertainers who regularly patronise the hotel. The **Soho Bar** in the **Piccadilly** pub (171 Victoria Street) is younger, less formal (to get in wear black, Darlinghurst's universal non-colour) and a good example of Sydney pub deco architecture.

Finally, Harold Park Hotel (115 Wigram Road, Glebe) has a stimulating 'Writers in the Park' evening every Tuesday. Some of Australia's best (and least) known writers read their works in this quintessentially Oz 'tiles-and-track' pub, located just adjacent to the Harold Park 'trots' (or harness racing track).

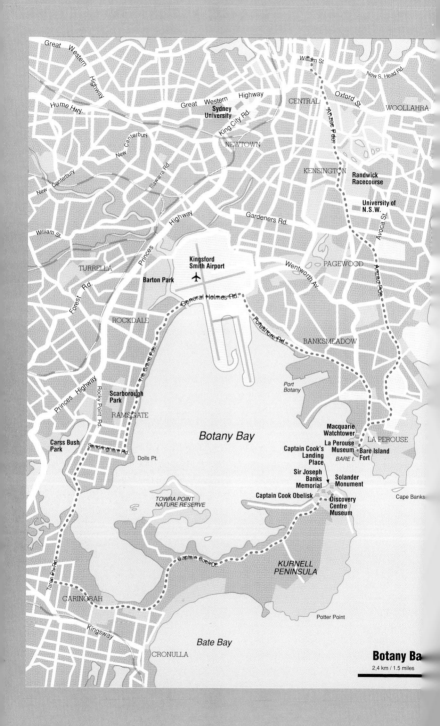

Great Western Highway

Hume Hwy.

New Canterbury

Illawarra Rd.

New Canterbury

William St.

William St.

New S. Head Rd.

Oxford St.

CENTRAL

WOOLLAHRA

Great Western Highway

Sydney University

King City Rd.

NEWTOWN

KENSINGTON

Randwick Racecourse

University of N.S.W.

Gardeners Rd.

Anzac Pde.

Oxford St.

Avoca St.

Highway

Princes

TURRELLA

Kingsford Smith Airport

Wentworth Av.

PAGEWOOD

Anzac Pde.

Forest Rd.

Barton Park

General Holmes Rd.

Foreshore Rd.

BANKSMEADOW

William St.

ROCKDALE

The Grand Pde.

Scarborough Park

Port Botany

RAMSGATE

Rocky Point Rd.

Sandringham Rd.

Botany Bay

Macquarie Watchtower

LA PEROUSE

La Perouse Museum

Bare Island Fort

Carss Bush Park

Dolls Pt.

Captain Cook's Landing Place

BARE I.

Sir Joseph Banks Memorial

Solander Monument

TOWRA POINT NATURE RESERVE

Captain Cook Obelisk

Discovery Centre Museum

Cape Banks

Taren Pde.

Captain Cook Dr.

KURNELL PENINSULA

CARINGBAH

Kingsway

Potter Point

CRONULLA

Bate Bay

Botany Ba

2,4 km / 1.5 miles

7. Botany Bay

Here's a chance to get out of the city (though not out of Sydney), to cross the great red-tiled suburban sea and to arrive, yet again, at the ocean. It's the perfect chance for a picnic, at either La Perouse or Kurnell. Combining wilderness, historical sites and a contemporary industrial 'frightscape', Botany Bay is where European Australia began, with Captain Cook and all that...

You'll need a car for this tour. Starting at **Taylor Square** (in Oxford Street), drive south from the city along ANZAC Parade. This long avenue passes a number of sacred sporting sites, the Sydney Cricket Ground, Moore Park Golf Course, Randwick Racecourse and the University of New South Wales. Through Maroubra, continue south until you hit **La Perouse** on the northern arm of Botany Bay. The 16-km (10-mile) drive from Sydney takes about 30 minutes.

Windswept **Botany Bay** is where European Australia hiccoughed to life, when, at 3pm on 29 April 1770, James Cook, RN, stepped ashore from the *Endeavour* to assay the 'Great South Land' for Britain. The place was named Botany Bay after more than 3,000 new botanical specimens were collected by the expedition's naturalist, Joseph Banks. Australia's most famous convict ballad, *Botany Bay*, was inspired by the fearful reputation of this place. In 1788, the First Fleet anchored here briefly, found the site unsuitable for a permanent settlement, and moved to Sydney Cove, a better-watered site on an excellent harbour that Cook had overlooked.

The **La Perouse Monument**, built in 1828, commemorates the 1788 visit by a small French fleet commanded by the explorer Comte de La Perouse, who arrived in Botany Bay only six days after Captain Arthur Phillip and the First Fleet had left. After sailing from Botany Bay, La Perouse's ships apparently disappeared off the face of the earth, until their wreckage was discovered in the Solomon Islands in 1828. The monument, the idea of Baron de Bougainville, who visited the site in 1825, is looked after by the NSW National Parks and Wildlife Service.

Kurnell: Where it all began

ANCHORING THE 'ENDEAVOUR'

In front of you out on the bay, approximately 500 metres away, there is a red buoy. This is the site where Captain James Cook anchored the 'Endeavour' in 1770.

The Maritime Services Board now maintains this site as one of its navigational markers for ships entering Botany Bay.

La Perouse Museum

The 1881 **Old Cable Station** (open daily 10am–4.30pm, tel: 96612765) at ANZAC Parade, La Perouse, was built to house the workers operating the 1876 undersea telegraph line to New Zealand, and now houses the **La Perouse Museum** and an **Aboriginal Art Gallery**. Nearby is the 1820s **Macquarie Watchtower**, the oldest building on the bay, erected by Governor Macquarie to house soldiers attempting to control smuggling in Botany Bay. A nearby grave is of Père Receveur, a Franciscan monk who was part of La Perouse's expedition.

On Sunday afternoon this is a lively area, with the local Aborigines, migrant families, picnickers and sightseers all enjoying the open space and fresh air. There is even a snake tamer's show (from 1.30pm) in the little metal enclosure near the last bus stop. Linked by a bridge to the shore is **Bare Island Fort**. The fort was constructed in 1881, in anticipation of French or Russian attacks, and its barracks were added in 1889. The foes did not materialise, so the guns have never been fired in anger.

On the southern arm of the bay, **Kurnell Peninsula**, now the home of huge oil refineries, is the site of **Captain Cook's Landing Place**. Located 36km (22 miles) south of Sydney, it is reached by driving from La Perouse along Foreshore Road, General Holmes Drive, the Grand Parade, Taren Point Road and Captain Cook Drive. The drive will take about 20 minutes, and can be broken by a drink at the **Resort Hotel Brighton**.

Several monuments commemorate the eight days Cook spent at Kurnell. These include the **Captain Cook Obelisk** (erected in 1870); **Sir Joseph Banks Memorial** (1947); **Solander Monument** (1914) and a tablet to the memory of **Seaman Forby Sutherland**,

Boomerangs at La Perouse

View of Botany Bay from Kurnell

the first European definitely known to be buried on the continent. All of these are more historical than spectacular, but the site is perfect for a quiet picnic, with views across the broad blue bay. A small rock just offshore of the Captain Cook Obelisk is the site of the first recorded white footfall on eastern Australia – that of seaman Isaac Smith.

The National Parks and Wildlife Service maintains the **Banks-Solander Track** and the **Discovery Centre** museum (Monday to Friday 10.30am–4.30pm, Saturday, Sunday and public holidays, 10.30am–5pm, tel: 96689923). Much of this part of the peninsula is good for easy bushwalks; the landscape is a combination of wide-open space, some bush and rocky coastal fringes.

Spare a thought as you wander around here for the Gwiyagal Aborigines who inhabited this rich area before the arrival of the *Endeavour* and all who followed. They would probably recognise the nearby **Towra Point Nature Reserve**, one of the last coastal wetland sanctuaries in Sydney for native and migratory birds. (Entry for humans these days, though, is by National Parks and Wildlife Service permit only.) The Gwiyagal Aborigines certainly wouldn't recognise the massive oil refinery that occupies much of the interior of the peninsula today.

There is plenty of opportunity to swim at beaches and baths around Botany Bay, from La Perouse to any number of points along **The Grand Parade** to **Dolls Point**, right around to Kurnell – but, beware of nasty sharks, especially during summer. Look for the meshed enclosures. While you're here, you might continue south to **Cronulla**, the city's southernmost and longest surf beach with its 10km (6 miles) of sand dunes stretching south from Kurnell.

Memorial at Kurnell

8. Darling Harbour

The most visited of Sydney's harbourside public areas, the Darling Harbour complex can take up as much time as you have. It is easily reached from the city via the convenient and fast monorail. Once there, you can just wander around and browse, or fill many hours at the Powerhouse Museum... or at the bars.

It is difficult to describe Darling Harbour because it has so many facets that each visitor sees it in a different light. And yet, to describe it as a collection of shops, restaurants, bars, museums, funfair, outdoor entertainment and marina, plus a convention centre, a huge exhibition hall, a Chinese garden and an entertainment centre on the fringe of the city does not quite give it the sense of identity the area is quickly developing. On Sunday, when the rest of Sydney

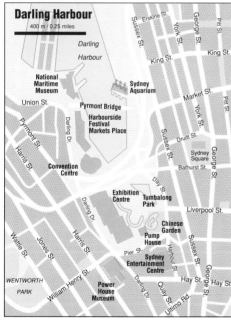

has largely shut down, Darling Harbour exudes good spirits and is crowded with locals and visitors alike.

Perhaps the best way to explain Darling Harbour – *the* success story of Australian urban renewal – is to put it in a brief historical context. For many years prior to its redevelopment, Darling Harbour fulfilled the role as Sydney's unwashed sink, an industrial eyesore comprising 50ha (123½ acres) of rail yards, wharfs and factories at Sydney's back door. Then, in 1984, the state premier promised that the area would be 'reborn' as a bicentennial gift to the people of Sydney in 1988. It was.

The Darling Harbour project was clouded in controversy. One aspect of the development was a monorail between the city and Darling Harbour. Detractors claim that the monorail has destroyed the appearance of the city and still wait for it to be torn down: its every breakdown and financial loss is eagerly reported in the press, but others find it a convenient link between the city and the harbour. And there is one element of Darling Harbour that almost didn't happen. Cynical Sydneysiders relate with glee how a proposed casino development is only now being developed because, for half a decade, the government couldn't find anyone honest to run it.

Suffice to say that, despite its incomplete state, there is a lot to see and do in Darling Harbour. Start at the **Sydney Aquarium** (open daily 9.30am–9pm, tel: 92622300) on the city side of the cove. Shaped like a breaking wave, the aquarium contains a good cross-section of the incredible range of fish that inhabit Australian waters. Although there are no crocodiles in New South Wales waters, visitors and locals who are not heading north to the tropics can see them here. Sydney certainly does have sharks, however, and nose-to-nose confrontations are reassuringly safe in the aquarium's transparent tunnel surrounded by the inhabitants of the harbour.

Pyrmont Bridge, right beside the aquarium, provides the fastest pedestrian access to Darling Harbour from the city. First built in 1858, the private toll bridge charged pedestrians 'tuppence' each way; sheep and pigs were charge a farthing a head. By the 1880s, the old wooden bridge had outlived its usefulness and the government suggested demolishing it to open up Darling Harbour.

The resulting public outcry was echoed a century later when the government considered tearing down its successor. Neither government went ahead. Instead, the colonial government bought the bridge and abolished the toll, later replacing the whole structure. When the Pyrmont Bridge that stands today was opened in 1902, the year after Australia became a nation, it was a hailed as a wonder that pushed the limits of contemporary engineering. The bridge, with its quaint control box in the middle, is worthy of inspection, its electronically-powered 800-tonne, 70-m (230-ft) 'swing span' pivots horizontally to allow large vessels to enter the inner harbour.

The **National Maritime Museum** (tel: 95527500), to the right of Pyrmont Bridge, houses all manner of vessels both as permanent outdoor displays and inside exhibits dealing with all facets of Australians' relationship with the sea. Nearby, there's a display of an old grain clipper and other lovely old craft.

Further down the water-

inese Garden, Darling Harbour

front are the shops, bars and restaurants of the **Harbourside Festival Market Place** (Monday to Saturday 10am–9pm, Sunday 10am–6pm). Styled after Fishermen's Wharf of San Francisco, this is an enormous speciality shopping centre with over 200 outlets.

Further down is the **Darling Harbour Convention Centre** (tel: 92825000). A seven-storey spiral edifice that seats up to 3,500 delegates, this is the largest of its kind in Australia. Next door, the **Exhibition Centre** (tel: 92825000), with an indoor area the size of five football fields without columns (and all the goals are commercial), is the preferred Sydney venue for trade shows displays from boats to cars to travel products – daily newspapers provide details.

Facing the Convention Centre is **Tumbalong Park**, a grassy circle fringed by eucalyptus and tree-lined walks radiating into the middle distance. The landscaping comprises mainly Australian vegetation. Catering for playtime for all ages there is both a children's playground and amphitheatre for open air performances. Buskers and bands perform here, particularly on sunny weekends.

Adjacent to the Tumbalong Park is the **Chinese Garden** (open daily 9.30am–7pm, tel: 92816863), built as a bicentennial gift by the government of China's Guangdong Province. It is found behind high walls protecting it from the noise pollution of the traffic flow. Inside, you'll find a peaceful garden refuge of lakes, waterfalls and perfectly executed landscaping.

The venerable **Pier Street Pump House** (Monday to Saturday 11am–midnight, Sunday noon–10pm, tel: 91291841), in Pump House Lane, which provided hydraulic pressure to operate lifts and bank vault doors around the city, is now a boutique brewery where you can drink beer while watching the next one being produced. This tavern is always crowded.

The **Entertainment Centre** (tel: 92112222 for information) straddles the division between Darling Harbour and Chinatown and is right opposite the Pump House. Many of the world's greatest stars have trodden the boards of the 'Ent Cent' and there seems to be no end to the flow – as long as Sydney's summer coincides with the cold northern winters. Again, newspapers detail forthcoming attractions. A 5-minute walk away, at 500 Harris Street, is the **Power House Museum** (open daily 10am–5pm, tel: 92170111), now the state's prime tourist attraction. The building started life as the power plant for Sydney's trams and has ended up as a hands-on celebration of arts, technology and social history. It is large enough to contain the whole Opera House and there are times when the daunted visitor feels that this edifice must be about the only thing not on display. There is something for everyone – from New South Wales' first passenger train engine, complete with three fitted-out carriages, to crafts and fashion, and a transport section with cars, planes and even a space shuttle. The emphasis is on things Australian, although the international context is not lost. This ongoing exposition by the Museum of Applied Arts and Sciences is a living museum of a people's achievements.

Right, Darling Harbour

9. Blue Mountains

Although some of the attractions of the Blue Mountains can be visited by a combination of rail and taxi, the best way to explore this area is by car. The mountains can fill anywhere from a day to a week. However, a full day is sufficient to give you a taste of what the area has to offer.

Seen from any Sydney vantage point, the thin line of the Blue Mountains on the western horizon looks far from impressive. The mountains are not very high. Indeed, **Mount Victoria**, on the Great Western Highway, the highest and coldest point in the range aspires to a mere 1,111m (3,645ft). However, this plateau is so deeply indented that it took 24 years for the first white settlers to find a way across the mountains to the pasture lands of the west.

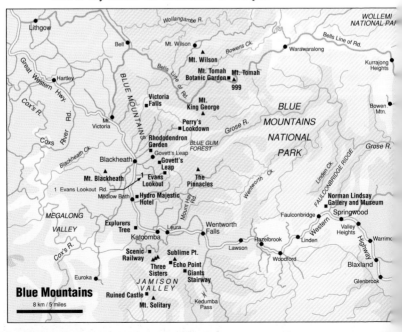

Blue Mountains: a grand vista of mountains, gorges and valleys

This results in unusual mountain terrain where most walks involve heading *down* from the road then back *up* to the car at the end of the day.

The Blue Mountains take their name from a trick of the light. When viewed from a distance, refracted light on minute droplets of eucalyptus oil in the atmosphere from the millions of gum trees which cover the mountains creates a blue haze. Popular with bush-walkers and rockclimbers, the area is part of one of New South Wales' largest national parks and provides surprisingly grand vistas and beautiful gorges and valleys. An added bonus is that when it is hot in Sydney the mountain glens are pleasantly cool. In winter, the cool temperatures, log fires and the occasional snowfall create a striking contrast to Sydney's temperate days.

In the 1870s, the Blue Mountains were regarded primarily as a holiday centre for Sydneysiders – a role it retained for several decades. However, by the 1970s, the Blue Mountains had fallen out of favour as a recreational area. Since then, the area has gone thorough a renaissance of sorts, and today, there are several new resorts, some highly regarded restaurants, and eucalyptus forest trails full of healthy walkers.

Katoomba, 100km (62 miles) west of Sydney, is the major tourist centre of the Blue Mountains and has been a holiday resort for more than a century. It is built on a series of hills that drop steeply into the **Jamison Valley**. The town is well served by electric trains from Sydney (about 90 minutes away) and is on the Great Western Highway. To orientate yourself, go straight to the tourist information centre at **Echo Point** (tel: 47-396266). A short trail leads to the point that provides a

Hardy walkers

The Three Sisters, Katoomba

magnificent view past the famous **Three Sisters** rock formation – a series of rocky pinnacles that feature in an Aboriginal legend – over Jamison Valley.

The nearby **Giants Stairway** descends by 1,000 steps to the valley floor, from where there are several walks of varying length and difficulty. Treks to the **Ruined Castle** and **Mount Solitary** from here will take most of the day, are fairly hard and require planning. Details of these, and many other walks, are available from the National Parks and Wildlife Service.

One of the easiest walks from the bottom of the stairway is to the right towards the base of the **Scenic Railway.** This enduring tourist attraction has operated safely for many years and was originally constructed in the 1880s to transport miners and coal up from the valley. This is a good point to bear in mind as you ascend a seemingly sheer cliff face on the flimsy contraption. Going down is worse: one has the terrifying sensation of plunging vertically 445m (1,460ft) down to the valley floor (in fact it's a 45 degree incline). If you enjoy scaring yourself, you should also do the **Orphan Rocker**, another cliff-top ride.

Leura, a town many regard as the prettiest village in the mountains, adjoins Katoomba and is reached by a scenic clifftop drive. Its historic main street has been restored and abounds with craft, antique and tea shops. Visit **Everglades Gardens** with its 5ha (12 acres) of landscaped grounds, and **Leuralla** (Wednesday to Sunday 10am–5pm, tel: 47-841169), once the home of Dr H V Evatt – the first president of the United Nations – a stately home built in 1914 in art deco style. The house includes a collection of 19th-century Australian art historical objects and a restaurant. After sightseeing, call in at the luxurious **Fairmont Resort** (tel: 47-825222) poised on the clifftop at Sublime Point, just outside of town.

The other upmarket resort in the mountains is **Lilianfels** at Echo Point, near Katoomba, an 85-room country retreat built around a historic 1890 home. A 2-acre ornamental garden, bushwalking tracks, stunning views of the Jamison valley and a quality restaurant are among the offerings. Call 47-810200 for more information. However, if the wallet doesn't allow it, there is variety of budget and bed-and-breakfast accommodation throughout the Blue Mountains area.

Continuing on the highway along the ridge top westwards from Katoomba, the road passes the **Explorers Tree**, commemorating the successful crossing of this seemingly impenetrable range by explorers Gregory Blaxland, William Lawson and William Wentworth in 1813. For the very adventurous, this is also the starting point for the **Six Foot Track**, a bushwalk that takes two to three days and ends at Jenolan Caves. Further on, stop at the **Hydro Majestic Hotel** at **Medlow Bath**. Built between 1880 and 1903, this extraordinary hotel is an Edwardian folly with art deco touches and a cavernous dining room that offers stunning views out over the Megalong Valley.

Blackheath is the next main town along the highway. Originally called Hounslow, the settlement was renamed by Macquarie upon his return from Bathurst in 1815 because of its black and wild look. The town grew up around the railway and was a favourite stopping place for 19th-century miners heading west to the gold diggings.

The local **Rhododendron Garden**, featuring more than 1,500 rhododendrons in a bush setting, is worth a visit, and the area has spectacular views of the tree-lined Grose Valley from **Evans Lookout** and **Govetts Leap**, which are also starting points for several bushwalks into the National Park.

The best introduction to the mountains is the **Grand Canyon walk**, a 3–4 hour hike that is not very taxing. Take the signposted road out to Evans Look-

A lush Blue Mountains' garden in spring

out where you leave the car and descend a fairly steep trail into the rainforest and canyon. The canyon itself is a narrow passage lined with ferns that opens up to a sunny shaded glen. Finally, you climb through a shaded glen to return to the road.

An alternative, more difficult walk is from **Perry's Lookdown** to

One of several picturesque golf courses in the Blue Mountains

the **Blue Gum Forest**. The only hard part of the walk is the descent to the valley floor and the climb out of the valley at the end of the day (either back to Perry's Lookdown or to Govetts Leap). The Blue Gum Forest with its crystal stream, grassy swathes and towering eucalyptus is an excellent goal for a day walk. Just make sure that you save some energy for the climb out.

From Blackheath, you can also drive down from the escarpment on the other side into the **Megalong Valley**, a tranquil farming area that offers horse riding excursions at the **Packsaddlers** (tel: 47-879150). On the way back to Sydney make a stop at the **Norman Lindsay Gallery and Museum** (Friday to Sunday and public holidays 11am–5pm, tel: 47-511067) at Faulconbridge. Lindsay was one of Australia's most acclaimed and notorious painters, as well as being a writer and sculptor of note. He lived in this stone cottage for 57 years up to his death in 1969. The house contains an important collection of his paintings, drawings, etchings (he specialised in twee scenes of voluptuous Bacchanalia), novels and ship models, now owned by the National Trust. The landscaped gardens include several of Lindsay's larger statues and fountains.

Also of interest in Faulconbridge is the **Prime Ministers' Corridor of Oaks**, in which a tree has been planted by every Australian Prime Minister or his family. This is also the gravesite of Sir Henry Parks, a five-time New South Wales premier and the father of the Australian Federation.

The only real reason to approach the mountains by the northern road (through Richmond, across the Nepean River and along the scenic Bell's Line of Road) is to visit the **Mount Tomah Botanic Garden**. This Bicentennial project is an offshoot of Sydney's Royal Botanic Gardens and displays temperate plants in a series of walking trails as well as a formal garden. A side excursion from here to **Mount Wilson** is worthwhile because high rainfall and rich volcanic soils have produced some exceptional private gardens which are open to the public in spring and autumn. (Check locations and dates at tel: 91279047 or 47-396266.) From Mount Wilson, there are panoramic views of the mountain range.

Rail buffs may wish to proceed towards Lithgow, a remarkably unattractive industrial and mining town set in a narrow valley on the western side of the range. Coal has been mined here since 1869 and new mines and a power station have grown up around the 19th-century buildings in the town's main street. The **Zig Zag Railway** (tel: 63-514826) is located a few kilometres short of Lithgow: it is a 13-km (8-mile) section of rail line ingeniously built in the 1860s to descend the western escarpment of the mountains. Rail enthusiasts operate the line at weekends (10.30am, 12.15pm, 2pm and 3.30pm) for tourists who wish to experience a steam train ride and early colonial engineering resourcefulness.

Jenolan Caves

If you have more than a day to spare up in the mountains, a turnoff from the Great Western Highway, just outside Hartley (130km from Sydney), will take you the 48km (30 miles) to **Jenolan Caves**, long renowned as Australia's most famous limestone cave system.

After passing through Hampton State Forest, you skirt the Kanangra Boyd National Park along a steep, winding road and eventually round a bend to be confronted by the surprising spectacle of the 24-m (79-ft) high **Grand Arch**. The road turns into this gaping cleft in the hillside and emerges outside the Tudor-style sandstone **Jenolan Caves House** (tel: 63-593311). Built at the turn of the century, Jenolan Caves House has attracted visitors since the caves were first opened to the public. Like much of the mountain facilities, it was looking seedy until a few years ago when new management renovated it to a high standard of comfort.

According to legend, the caves were first discovered by white settlers during the pursuit of a bushranger in 1838. Almost 30 years later they were opened to the public. Now there are six cavern systems open. These caverns contain an amazing diversity of formations – stalactites, stalagmites, paper-thin 'straws' and other strangely contorted shapes – all created by the action of air on dripping limestone-bearing water. The entire cave system forms a massive underground labyrinth of which the readily accessible few are only a tiny portion. Some of the caves can be explored without a guide, others may only be visited as part of a regular tour. You should wear sound walking shoes with a good grip and prepare for quite a lot of climbing up and down of steps.

Jenolan Caves

71

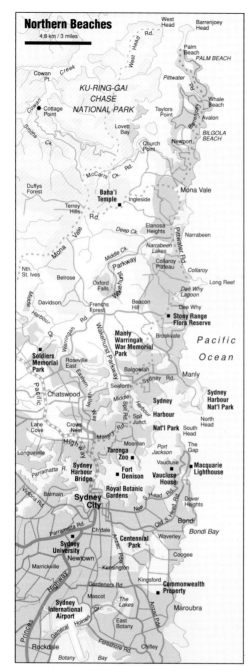

Northern Beaches

4.8 km / 3 miles

10. Northern Beaches

The finger of land that points north to Palm Beach, bounded by the Pacific Ocean on one side and Pittwater on the other, is the heartland of Sydney's surfing culture. To explore the hedonistic flipside of Sydney's urban lifestyle, all you need is a car and a spare day, preferably at the weekend.

From the city, the first part of this journey takes you across the Sydney Harbour Bridge, along the boutique shopping strip of Neutral Bay and Mosman's Military Road then across the Spit Bridge. Continue following the signs to Narrabeen and Palm Beach. A little past Dee Why, 19km from the city, the road first parallels and then opens out to a view of the Pacific coast. At the end of Dee Why lagoon, you'll see **Long Reef Point** and one of the world's most scenic golf courses – it takes up the whole headland and a wide rock shelf at water level. Turn right into Anzac Avenue at the end of the golf course and drive up to the lookout. From this vantage point the coastal topography is immediately apparent. The Sydney coastline is a series of headlands scalloped by beautiful sheltered beaches. The houses on these vantage points have incredibly panoramic views and comprise some of the city's most desirable real estate.

From here, the beach suburbs read like a litany from the daily surf reports on Sydney radio: Collaroy, Narrabeen, Bungan, Warriewood, Mona Vale, Newport, Bilgola, Avalon, Whale Beach and Palm Beach. Select one that appeals to you and stop for a swim. If there are red and yellow flags up, swim between them and risk ending up with a surfboard wedged in your ear. The flagged areas will be patrolled in summer by a lifesaver. One of the prettiest of the northern beaches is **Bilgola** on the peninsula – turn right at the top of the ridge after Newport and drive down to the car park. This is the location of a small community snuggled into the diminutive rainforested cove far below Barrenjoey Road.

Continuing on to **Palm Beach**, the peninsula flattens out before rising to **Barrenjoey** ('baby kangaroo') **lighthouse**, picturesquely perched 113m (371ft) above the waters of Broken Bay, at the very tip of the peninsula. Palm Beach is the favoured address of media personalities, film industry folk and anyone else who doesn't have to drive into the city every day.

By now it should be lunchtime. There are a number of options here. To really drop into the spirit of things you should buy (at Newport, Avalon or Palm Beach) some prawns or fish and chips wrapped in newspaper, and eat them on a beach.

There are several good restaurants at Palm Beach. **Barrenjoey House** (1108 Barrenjoey Road, tel: 99744001) is expensive but its Australian/French food is almost as good as its setting. However, Sydney's foodies recommend nearby **Beach Road Restaurant** (1 Beach Road, tel: 99141159) as a good combination of reasonable prices, great location and excellent food. There is yet another option, one which qualifies as a Sydney institution. Retrace your steps to the **Newport Arms** (Kalinya Street, Newport, tel: 99974900) on Pittwater, a legendary northside hotel. Although there are cheaper places to buy lunch and much easier places to find parking, a pub lunch in the beer garden of the Newport Arms during summer is a chance to drop straight into Sydney's surfing and sailing cultures.

Palm Beach and Barrenjoey headland

Northern beaches panorama

To return to the city, drive south to Mona Vale, then, turning inland, take Mona Vale Road along the coastal highlands. Set high in the bushland and commanding a spectacular view 4km (2½ miles) from the coast is the imposingly exotic **Baha'i Temple** at Ingleside that is open to the public. If you have time, turn into McCarr's Creek Road and then into **Ku-ring-gai National Park** and along to **West Head**. This park of 14,712ha (36,339 acres) was dedicated in 1894 to preserve an example of Sydney's original landscape. With luck you may see a koala here. In any case, the views over Pittwater from the **West Head** lookout are worth the detour. There are many walking trails in the park, ranging from short strolls to full day outings to secluded beaches. If you wish to take to the water rather than merely overlook it, there are boat hiring facilities at **Akuna Bay** and **Bobbin Head**.

Return to Mona Vale Road, turn right and follow the signs to the Pacific Highway (about 20 minutes), then turn left on the Highway and head to the city (about 30 minutes). This takes you through a cross-section of the affluent northern suburbs (known collectively and misleadingly as 'the North Shore') whose descriptions are invariably prefixed with the adjective 'leafy'. It's not hard to see why.

11. Hawkesbury River Cruise

Take a day trip out to the Hawkesbury River to the north of Sydney. The suburbs don't quite reach this far – but you can join the last Australian mail riverboat run, dropping supplies to isolated communities along the river.

Although picturesque **Brooklyn** is less than an hour by car from Sydney, the best way to get there is by train. Stepping on the air-conditioned inter-city train at Central Railway and stepping off only a short walk from the riverboat wharf certainly beats fighting against the northern suburbs' morning traffic. At main stations like Central you can buy a combined rail and mailboat ticket – it's not cheaper, just more convenient.

There was a time when much of Australia's mail was carried by river. However, the development of road and rail has reduced that flow to a single trickle: the **Hawkesbury Riverboat Postman**. There are several small communities found along the Hawkesbury that are only accessible by water; others use boats to eliminate a long, circuitous drive. Letters are not all that the little mailboat carries: it delivers everything from eggs and milk to building supplies.

An idyllic way to kill time (or bring to life) a day is a ride on the Riverboat Mail Run which departs Brooklyn at 9.30am each weekday (except public holidays) and returns around 1.15pm. On Wednesday and Friday it also completes an afternoon run, leaving at 1.30pm and returning at about 4.15pm. To allow plenty of time, you should catch the 8.09am train from Central Railway. A smorgasbord lunch is available on board the boat or you can wait to have lunch at one of the cafes or hotel at Brooklyn upon your return. The fare includes morning or afternoon tea. It's a good idea to book the cruise in advance a day or so. Bookings and inquiries at tel: 99857566.

Baha'i Temple, Ingleside

Apart from the oddity value of participating in an aquatic mail run, this trip is a good way to see one of the most attractive areas of bushland in the Sydney region. Much of the area remains heavily forested with eucalyptus, most of it national park reserve, while the

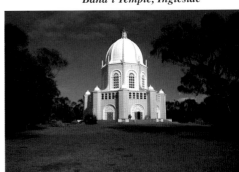

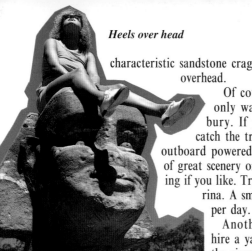

characteristic sandstone crags of Hawkesbury River tower overhead.

Of course, the mail run is not the only way to experience the Hawkesbury. If you have the time, drive or catch the train to Brooklyn, then hire an outboard powered dinghy. This promises a day of great scenery on safe water, plus a little fishing if you like. Try Dori's Boats or Baymac Marina. A small boat will cost about A$60 per day.

Another worthwhile option is to hire a yacht or houseboat and explore the river over several days. More than 20 charter outlets operate from Pittwater (Newport, Bayview and Church Point), Brooklyn, Bobbin Head, Akuna Bay and, much further upstream, from Wisemans Ferry. Boats range from yachts of all varieties to motor cruisers and luxury houseboats. Some recommended operators include Skipper a Clipper (tel: 94501888) and Hawkesbury Water Ways Hire Cruisers (tel: 94562866). The long-established Halvorsens (tel: 94579011) is good for motor cruisers. Try the Perfect Escape Boat Hire (tel: 99973444) for sailing craft and Fenwicks Marina (tel: 99857633) for the flat-bottomed variety.

If you like, you don't have to take to the water at all to see the Hawkesbury. Much of this deep, sheltered waterway is bounded by national parks – coastal Bouddi and Brisbane Waters, and the rug-

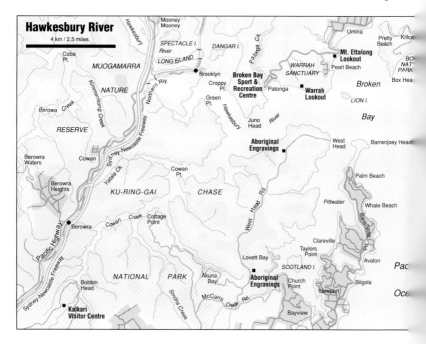

Hawkesbury River Bridge, Brooklyn

ged wilderness of Dharug, Marramarra and Ku-ring-gai Chase. Camping is permitted in most of the five national parks, but conditions vary from basic bush camping to fully-equipped sites. It is best to check with the National Parks and Wildlife Service office at Cadman's Cottage, 110 George Street, Sydney, tel: 92478861.

12. Royal National Park

The Royal National Park at Sutherland is the second oldest national park in the world. While it may lack a sense of real outback wilderness, it has the decided advantage of being the city's most accessible bushland.

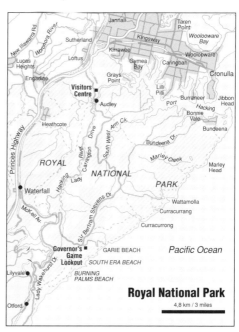

The **Royal National Park** at Sutherland, on the southern limits of Sydney, had a historical role of global significance. It was created in 1879 and is the second oldest public reserve in the world – only Yellowstone in the United States (formed in 1872) is older. However, the Royal was the world's first 'national park' (a title that was also subsequently given to Yellowstone in 1883). The Sydney park later had a name change – the

A waterfront community nestled around the Royal National Park

'Royal' tag was bestowed by Queen Elizabeth during a visit to Sydney in 1954.

With the establishment of this and Yellowstone, the concept of natural areas set aside for public use was born. However, the idea of preserving native bush was far from the thoughts of the park's founders. While national parks are regarded today as areas where the natural environment is preserved in perpetuity, this park was intended as a pleasure ground modelled after London's Hampstead Heath. Some of the Australian bush was torn out to be replaced by imported plants and manicured lawns. Until 1922, the trust for this 15,000-ha (37,065-acre) region earned an income from logging. Rabbits and foxes were introduced, and Javanese rusa deer and fallow deer released into the park in the late 1890s are still there.

Although the park still lacks a feeling of pristine wilderness in the most well-frequented areas, several regions of attractive bushland can be found by anyone prepared to walk. Bounded by Port Hacking to the north, the Pacific Ocean to the east and the railway line to the west, the Royal National Park is predominantly a heath-covered sandstone plateau. However, the valleys are full of rainforests, with a luminous green luxuriance of buttress roots, liana vines and innumerable ferns. The native animals are timid and most are nocturnal so visitors don't see them with the same frequency as the 200 bird types that inhabit the park.

Within the park's dense grottoes one may hear a whip bird (its call sounds like a stock whip being cracked) or see the exquisite lyre bird, named after its lyre-shaped tail. Look out for the satin bower bird: it looks like a raven at first glance but a closer look reveals that the bird's plumage is a deep iridescent mauve.

The Royal National Park is easy to reach from Sydney by road or public transportation. If driving, just follow the Princes Highway for about 45 minutes to the turnoff into the park at **Loftus**. The alternative for train travellers is to travel along the Illawarra line and disembark at one of the several stations around or within the park (Waterfall, Helensburg or Otford) then walk in. Or you can take a train to Cronulla (tel: 95420648), then a ferry across Port Hacking to **Bundeena**. The main visitor centre and wildlife shop (open daily 9am–4pm) is at **Audley** where you will find plenty of information about the park. Or you can obtain some brochures in advance from the National Parks and Wildlife Service office in Cadman's Cottage, 110 George Street, Sydney, tel: 92478861.

There are over 150km (90 miles) of walking trails and numerous picnic and barbecue facilities within the park. You can rent canoes or paddleboats at Audley.

The roads through the Royal are not just day access routes: several are through roads between the south coast and Sydney (although the Princes Highway to Wollongong skirts the park's western boundary), and the Bundeena Road provides the only road access to Bundeena fishing village. **Lady Carrington Drive** that follows the Hacking River valley is flat and wide, and closed to traffic, so it's good for cycling and walking.

Along the shores of the park are 21km (13 miles) of coastline; surfing beaches interspersed by rugged sandstone headlands. The beaches at **Era, Burning Palms** and **Garie** are the most popular surfing beaches and **Bundeena** is a renowned windsurfing area. The well-appointed camping area of **Bonnie Vale** nearby is adjacent to a sandy spot which is good for swimming. **Wattamolla** has a good swimming lagoon and attracts many snorkellers and divers keen to explore the inlet.

Wilderness at the Royal National Park

Shopping

There's much more to shopping in Sydney than opals and boomerangs. The shopping suggestions on the next few pages cover a range of consumptions, but stops short of that favourite export of many Asian tourists – freezer packs of prime Aussie beef. The only limits to your cleaning out the shelves are your budget and (sigh) excess baggage allowance. Retail trading hours in Sydney are generally from 9am to 5.30pm on weekdays, except on Thursday evenings when shopping hours extend till 9pm. Hours are more varied on Saturday afternoon and Sunday is generally comatose except for large department stores which open from 10am to 4pm. Darling Harbour Marketplace is open until 9pm every night. Some bookshops (like Ariel at 42 Oxford Street, Paddington) are open till late, and sometimes all weekend. Chinatown shops are open daily from 8.30am to 6pm, if not later.

If you find a purchase (of opals or anything else) is faulty, take it back for an exchange or refund (always keep your receipts). New South Wales has clear consumer protection laws, and if you experience difficulties with the vendor, call the Department of Business and Consumer Affairs at tel: 92668911.

Australiana

'Australiana' covers a multitude of sins and skins. Americans (who have enough beef at home) tend to stock up on Akubra felt hats and Driza Bone oilskin coats for the 'Man from Snowy River' look, while, with all that frozen beef, the Japanese departure is more like the 'Man from Snowy Liver'. Many stores stock Australian rural gear, but the most famous one is **R M Williams** (389 George Street and elsewhere), because the old living legend, 'R M' himself, designed, wears and still manufactures much of it. **Thomas Cook Boot & Clothing** (790 George Street) carries a large range of High Country gear. Less macho garments can be found at various **Ken Done** shops (Darling Harbour, Skygarden, QVB,

Quintessentially, Australia

The Rocks), an Australian designer whose art is both wearable and ubiquitous. **Jenny Kee**, in the Strand Arcade, is the home of the designer's distinctly Australian hand-knit designs in sweaters, tops and scarves. For sheepskin products, try **Aries** (273 George Street).

Non-wearable Australiana and souvenirs can be purchased at gift shops in the **Australian Museum** (corner of William and College streets), the **Botanical Gardens**, **Art Gallery of New South Wales**, the **Sydney Opera House**, and National Trust historic buildings like **Juniper Hall** at 248 Oxford Street in Paddington.

Australiana also encompasses items of feral kitsch, from koala, kangaroo and sheep doorstops to more utilitarian items like stationery and household gadgets to unbearably fluffy koalas (made in Taiwan), fur purses, boomerangs and T-shirts. Of the sheepskin items, lambskin underlays for beds and cots are the best (and most sensible) buys. The **Perth Mint Shop** (corner of Druitt and York streets) has everything golden – from gold plated jewellery to solid gold coins. One

Skygarden on Pitt Street Mall

clever souvenir idea is a watch with a face made out of a coin from the date of your birth for less than A$200.

Popular tourist shopping beats are **The Rocks**, **Chinatown**, **Darling Harbour** (Harbourside Festival Marketplace) and **Birkenhead Point** (at Drummoyne). The Central Business District area boun-

A wet Oxford Street keeps the crowds away

ded by Hunter, Park, Clarence and Elizabeth streets sees most of the retail and duty-free shopping action by Sydneysiders. It contains, among others, **Centrepoint**, the **Imperial Arcade**, **Mid-City Complex**, **Strand Arcade**, **Skygarden** and **Queen Victoria Building**. All of these house scores of speciality gift, clothing, book, music, jewellery and craft and art shops. Beyond the city area, the suburbs renowned for power purchasing include **Mosman**, **Neutral Bay** and **Chatswood** (all north of the Bridge) and **Paddington**, **Bondi Junction** and **Double Bay** to the east of the city. **Remo General Store** (corner of Oxford and Crown streets, Darlinghurst) specialises in quality gifts, clothing and furnishings. **Sax Leather** (110A Oxford Street) has very good sandals and belts. **Skygarden** (77 Castlereagh Street) is as light and elevated as its name suggests. Six floors of parquetry, boutiquery, taste, tiles, 'name' apparel and galleries.

The **'Golden Square'** corner of King, Castlereagh and Elizabeth streets packs in a little ghetto of excellence: Celine and Chanel, Lowe and Louis Vuitton, etc, at their elegant best. Close by is Sydney's favourite department store, **David Jones** (known universally as 'DJs'), billed as 'the most beautiful store in the world'. There are two DJs emporia, at Elizabeth Street and Market Street, the former the more elegant, the latter with a basement Food Hall filled with scrumptious food. For market bargains and fun, the **Paddington Village Bazaar**, held on Saturdays in the Uniting Church in Oxford Street, is a rainbow mix of people and products: homemade jams and preserves, clothes by young fashion designers, jewellery, art and sculpture, second-hand clothes, books and other collectibles.

Have a Beary Christmas!

82

Opals

Many jewellery shops in the central shopping district (particularly in Pitt and Castlereagh streets) sell Australian opals and sapphires, either set or loose. Look for 'black' opals (with deeper colours, green and blue and nearly always sold as a thin wafer of opal between a dark backing and a transparent cap) and 'white' opals (a light background shot through with colours, normally sold as a solid stone). **Michal's** of Double Bay, **Rocks Opal Mine** (Clocktower Square, The Rocks), **E Gregory Sherman**, **Opals Australia, Madsen Opals** and **Gemtec** in the city are but a few reputable places to buy opals. Good opals are not cheap, and there is plenty of competition, so compare products and prices first.

Aboriginal Art

Bark paintings are the most common form of Koori (Aboriginal) art, but also consider contemporary works on board, or carved boomerangs and didgeridoos. Prices for paintings can range from A$100 to thousands. Try the **Aboriginal Art Centre**, 7 Walker Lane, Paddington, or in The Rocks at the Argyle Centre and the Clock Tower Building. **Coo-ee Aboriginal Art Gallery**, at 98 Oxford Street, claims to stock one of Australia's largest selection of Aboriginal arts and crafts.

Food

Besides slabs of frozen beef, local delicacies include macadamia nuts, bush honey, royal jelly, chocolates and the inevitable Vegemite, a savoury spread. The **David Jones Food Hall** downstairs in the Market Street store carries a good range. Australian wines can be purchased at any pub or bottle shop, with fair quality wines starting at A$10 per bottle. The flag bearer of Australian wines is an exquisite albeit expensive red: Penfolds Grange Hermitage.

Paddington Bazaar for the unexpected

Eating Out

There has been a remarkable change in Sydney, and indeed Australia, over the past decade or so. It has gone from being a gastronomical desert to one of the world's foremost culinary innovators. Much of the credit for this must rest with the waves of immigrants that have flowed into the country, bringing their national cuisines and respect for the fine art of food preparation with them. Australia, with its selection of fruit and vegetables from tropical to temperate and excellent farm produce, has always had excellent ingredients. It now cooks them well, too.

To experience the best in Australian cuisine, one that straddles the globe from Lyon to Bangkok, with passing acknowledgement to Rome and Beijing, you should visit at least one of Sydney's top restaurants. Expect the food to be exemplary, the service less so. Also on the downside are the rapid rises and falls that characterise Sydney restaurants: by the time you read this, the scene will have changed. Even so, the restaurants selected here have established some continuity and look set to carry on the same standards. Be warned that outside Australia's capital cities, restaurant offerings are likely to hark back to the 1950s-style 'bangers and mash' or 'meat and two veg' meals.

It is beyond the scope of this book to cover the many thousands of restaurant offerings in Sydney: the gourmet gospel is the *Good Food Guide* published annually by the *Sydney Morning Herald*. The alternative is *Cheap Eats in Sydney*, available at any newsagent. *Bon appetit!*

A bright and cheery table setting

The cost of a meal for two (without drinks) is categorised as follows: $=A$30 or less, $$=A$31–$50, $$$=A$51 or more.

The Finest Restaurants

The most spectacular restaurant setting in Australia is matched only by the quality of its food. The **Bennelong** ($$$, open for dinner Monday to Saturday 7–11pm, tel: 92507578), occupying prime position at the Sydney Opera House at Bennelong Point, was recently taken over by Gay Bilson and Janni Kyritsis, formerly of Berowra Waters Inn, for many years the most acclaimed restaurant in Australia. Brilliantly conceived dishes, perfectly executed, raises their meals to the realms of a gastronomic experience.

Claude's ($$$, open for dinner Tuesday–Saturday, tel: 93312325) at Woollahra is an excellent French restaurant in the Eastern Suburbs. It's small and intimate, and has a BYO policy – bring-your-own (bottle of whatever) – but there is nothing offhand about the quality of the food or service. Claude's is a venue for serious gourmet dining – eat, drink and enjoy.

Down in The Rocks, Neil Perry's **Rockpool** ($$$, open for lunch Monday–Friday and

Hard Rock Cafe, Crown Street

dinner Monday–Saturday, tel: 92521888) is, as the name suggests, a seafood restaurant. It's the best restaurant in Sydney to see how good Australia's ocean bounty can taste when it is well prepared. If the 'foodies' have moved on by the time you arrive, consider yourself lucky. If you're on a tight budget, try the Rockpool's **Oyster Bar**.

There are two very upmarket restaurants in Sydney that epitomise how well modern Australian cuisine melds cooking styles from around the world. **Darley St Thai** ($$$, open daily for dinner and lunch Tuesday–Sunday, tel: 93586530) at 30 Bayswater Road, Kings Cross, serves the nation's best Thai prepared by David Thompson. **Tetsuya's** at 729 Darling Street, Roselle ($$$, open for lunch Wednesday–Saturday and dinner Tuesday–Saturday, tel: 95551017), is where Tetsuya Wakuda combines French and Japanese cooking to produce the most exciting meals imaginable.

Harbourside Restaurants

If you regard a meal as requiring more than food alone, there are many Sydney restaurants that provide a spoon with a view. Sadly, Sydney has not been well served by harbourside restaurants. At many, the trade-off is spectacular views but mediocre food.

By dint of hard promotion over many years, **Doyles on the Beach** ($$$, open daily for lunch and dinner, tel: 93372007) has become a Sydney institution. There is no disputing the glorious setting – you look straight down the harbour to the bridge – but it is also a very expensive fish-and-chip restaurant. Next door is a cheaper alternative – the beer garden of the Doyle's **Watsons Bay Hotel** ($$, tel: 93374299).

Most of Sydney's picturesque restaurants are on the waterfront. The **Bathers Pavilion** ($$$, open daily for lunch and dinner, tel: 99681133) has a great location overlooking Balmoral Beach: ask for a window table. After the meal, a promenade walk along the beautiful waterfront can develop into a love affair with Sydney. Further north of town, **Freshwater Restaurant** ($$$, open daily for lunch and dinner, tel: 99385575) on Harbord Beach (also known as Freshwater Beach) is a beautiful spot on a sunny day. Food and service are both good and the daytime views energising.

There are some upmarket restaurants around The Rocks' waterside. **Bilsons** at the International Passenger Terminal ($$$, open for lunch and dinner Monday–Friday, dinner only Saturday and Sunday, tel: 92515600) and **No 7 at the Park** ($$$, open daily for lunch and dinner, tel: 92561630) at the Park Hyatt Hotel are both expensive and one suspects this is largely a viewpoint surcharge.

On the western side of the bridge and on the northern side of the harbour stands **Sails Harbourside** ($$$, open for lunch and dinner Monday–Saturday, lunch only on Sunday, tel: 99555793) at McMahons Point. Meals and service can both be erratic but the view across the water to the city is exceptional.

Also on the 'wrong' side of the bridge, but this time on the city side of the harbour, at the end of Pier 4, Walsh Bay, is the **Wharf** restaurant ($$$, open for lunch and dinner Monday–Saturday, tel: 92501761). The food is very good, the setting superb (especially on the outside deck in summer) and the prices are moderate. It is not plush but provides one of Sydney's best waterside dining experiences. It is also adjacent to the foyer of the Wharf Theatre, so consider combining dining with some good Sydney Theatre Company drama or comedy.

Although you won't find it in many guidebooks, there is another restaurant overlooking the harbour that merits a visit. The **Indian Empire** at 5 Walker Street, North Sydney ($$, tel:

Freshwater Restaurant

99232909), is an unpretentious Indian eatery that just happens to have spectacular views over the harbour. However, for very good Indian food, try the **Flavour of India** restaurants in Glebe ($$, tel: 96920662) or Edgecliff ($$, tel: 93262659).

High-Rise Restaurants

The best way to appreciate Sydney over a meal is to eat in a high-rise. Despite justifiable reservations about the quality of the cuisine at these eyrie restaurants (with the notable exception of Forty One), every visitor to Sydney should visit one of these high-altitude restaurants once. From a vantage point high above the city, Sydney's unique topography is laid out like a 3-D road map. Watch aircraft land at Mascot, boats sail the harbour and gaze at the Blue Mountains in the distance from your lofty perch, and by the end of the meal, the layout of the city will make sense for the first time.

There are several options where food and views combine but only one has recently won praise from food critics. **Forty One Restaurant** at Level 41 Chifley Tower ($$$, tel: 92212500) looks right down the harbour and beyond the heads towards New Zealand. As it was the state finalist for Restaurant of the Year in 1994, you can expect the food and atmosphere to be as refined as the view is wonderful.

Of course, Sydney does not escape the revolving tower restaurant – a.k.a 'pie-in-the-sky' dining. The **Summit** ($$$, open daily for lunch and dinner, tel: 92479777) is on top of Australian Square. The food and service is fair but you are really paying for the view. You have a choice of two **Sydney Tower** restaurants (open daily for lunch and dinner, tel: 92333722) at the revolving top of the tower above Centrepoint: an *à la carte* ($$$) or self service ($). Accept that the view is more important than the food here and choose the cheaper self service venue, reminiscent of lunch-at-mum's.

Ethnic Dining

Most of the previous pages have dealt with the sort of restaurant that the average Sydneysider would go to once or twice a year for a special occasion. The other side of the coin are restaurants that locals go to several times a week. Typically, many will be Asian and main courses will cost about A$10. Without a clearly defined Australian cuisine, Sydney has developed what may be the world's best array of international cuisines within a single city. Forty pages of restaurant listings in the Yellow Pages directory include a 'cuisine guide' with 35 headings from African to Vietnamese. For the past few years, Thai has definitely been the flavour in favour.

At this level, it's hard to differentiate between the masses of restaurants available. You are unlikely to have a brilliant meal but you have to be unlucky to have a bad one. This is the true success of the Sydney restaurant scene: no matter where you go, expect food that is better and cheaper than most countries in the world. Nor is this restricted to the centre – there are cheap eateries throughout the city and suburbs.

Nightlife

'The night is young' takes on a literal meaning in some Sydney scenes, as if there are invisible age barriers (and very visible fashion barriers) to mixing. In some of the clubs and rock pubs you won't feel too comfortable if you are over 30; in other places if you are under 30. Singles (both gay and straight) and couples are welcome at most of the following nightspots. In Sydney, the definition of a woman's night on the town is not necessarily 'dances with wolves'. Still, single women are pestered no more than in comparable cities – ie, too often for their liking.

Dress codes vary, from *de rigueur* designer fashion to 'neat casual'. Rest assured that sloppy or dirty clothing will often keep you out on the street. If you are one of the fortunate few who look eternally young, you must have identification to prove that you are over 18 (the minimum legal drinking age). For up-to-date listings of places, consult Friday's *Sydney Morning Herald* entertainment supplement, 'Metro', or free music papers like *Culture*, *Drum Media*, *Icon* and *3-D*.

Kings Cross Hotel

Clubs and Discos

Like their own butterfly clientele, some nightclubs have a brief, intense lifespan, and may not be there, at least by the same name, next time you look. The action heats up after 10.30pm, although many clubs have restaurant facilities for earlier dining. Cover charges vary from nothing to A$10 and upwards, depending upon who you are or know, how you dress, the night of the week – and

Harry's Cafe de Wheels, Woolloomoolo

the whim of the door prefect. As opening times vary, call first. The following are highly recommended:

Kinsela's (Bourke and Campbell streets, Taylor Square, tel: 93316200) has food, booze and boom. Designer decor, and a Thai restaurant. It used to be a funeral parlour, but people in black are still dying to get in. Open until 3am on most nights.

Hard Rock Cafe (121 Crown Street, Darlinghurst, tel: 93311116) is cloned from namesakes in too many other countries. Rock litter adorns the bar. Expect glamorous door queues (not unlike a bus stop), but good burgers and huge servings – though conversation gets decibelled to death.

Studebakers (19 Bayswater Road, Kings Cross, tel: 93585656) is another chain clone. Big, bright, new, groovy and popular with tourists and locals. A buffet is included in the entrance fee. Catch the bright red 1951 classic Bulletnose Studey in the foyer.

The Cauldron (207 Darlinghurst Road, Kings Cross, tel: 93311523) is packed with a largely single, horny, professional crowd. Its tiny dance floor guarantees a lot of personal contact.

Mr Goodbar (11 Oxford Street, Paddington, tel: 93606759) has a restaurant, bar, pool room, live music, etc.

Sight Bar (171 Victoria Street, Kings Cross, tel: 93586511) is next door to the popular Soho Bar. Dress sharp for the industrial wasteland decor. Models and fashion editors are especially welcome.

Bobby McGee's (377 Harbourside Festival Marketplace, Darling Harbour, tel: 92813944) is a fine, roaring joint in which to be young and in lust, or even a little older and in love, is acceptable. Beer, loud music, the crush of bodies, and great water views.

Club Deja Vu (252 Pitt Street, tel: 92618899) is a fashionable dance club with bars, pool tables and chillout rooms. Expect techno and ambient music.

Sugareef (20 Bayswater Road, Kings Cross, tel: 93585228) opens till late every night. Other dance clubs include **Rogues** (Oxford Square, Oxford Street, Darlinghurst, tel: 93321718) and **Blackmarket** (111 Regent Street, Chippendale, tel: 96988863).

Major hotels have their own clubs, such as **Juliana's** at the Sydney Hilton (259 Pitt Street) and **William's** at the Sydney Boulevard (90 William Street).

Rock

Social stratification by doorperson is less prevalent in rock pubs. All major live rock venues can be found listed in the Friday's *Sydney Morning Herald* 'Metro' section.

The Nag's Head pub (162 St John's Road, Glebe, tel: 96601591). Live music from Wednesday to Sunday.

Metro (624 George Street, tel: 92642666) features Indie rock, dance and live acts.

Lucy's Tavern (54 Castlereagh Street, tel: 92213908) attracts an office crowd as the work-a-day week crawls to an end. The music (and clientele) get louder as the evening progresses.

Studebakers Club, Kings Cross

The **Woolloomooloo Bay Hotel** (2 Bourke Street, Woolloomooloo, tel: 93571928) has live bands, good crowds throughout the weekend, and is popular day and night.

The **Rocks Rhythmboat** (tel: 92472979) departs from Pier One, Walsh Bay, at 7.30pm on Friday and Saturday nights. Offers live music/disco and dinner cruises on the harbour.

Selinas at the Coogee Bay Hotel (tel: 96650000), on the southern beach strip, features local bands and major touring acts.

Jazz

There is a healthy jazz scene, both traditional and contemporary.

Real Ale Cafe (66 King Street, City, tel: 92623277) has great food, drink and music. Live jazz nightly.

The **Rocks Rhythmboat** (tel: 92472979) has a jazz cruise on Sunday from noon to 4pm, departing from Pier 1, Hickson Road, Walsh Bay. Top jazz and blackboard menu.

Round Midnight (2 Roslyn Street, Kings Cross, tel: 93564045) is good for late-night jazz and blues. Comfortable ambience. As the name says, not much happening until after 11pm.

Strawberry Hills Hotel (453 Elizabeth Street, tel: 96982997) has good old traditional jazz on most nights.

The **Basement** (29 Reiby Street, Circular Quay, tel: 92512797) is the best blues and jazz supper venue in town. Open most nights and features quality local and overseas performers. Book a table if you're planning to do dinner and the show.

Both **Soup Plus** (383 George Street, tel: 91297728) and the **Harbourside Brasserie** (Pier One, Hickson Road, The Rocks, tel:

92523000) are versatile, friendly places, quality jazz oriented, and serve more than passable fare.

Coffee Stops

Adjacent to Kings Cross is Darlinghurst ('Darlo'/'Darling-it-hurts'), *the* place for heart-starter coffee. Along Victoria Street (heading south, away from the mêlée of the Cross), **Andiamo**, **Ditto**, **Tropicana**, **Morgans**, **Nicolina's**, **Back Door**, **Trivia**, **Bar Coluzzi**, **Unas** and **TJs**, along with **Michaelangelo's** (corner of William and Darlinghurst streets) and **Cafe Hernandez** (60 Kings Cross Road), all serve coffee of great conviction; most also serve good meals.

A 10-minute walk west, down towards the Central Business District, in Stanley Street (between Crown and Riley streets) in East Sydney, are more cafes (such as **Bill and Tony's**) which offer the same Italianate acceleration in addition to a pasta ballast.

For a quirky midnight snack (anyone for coffee with a meat pie chaser?), check out the famous **Harry's Cafe de Wheels** on the Woolloomooloo waterfront at Cowper Wharf Road. Look for a caravan up on the pavement, surrounded by nighthawks and cabs parked on the traffic island. And make sure you bring cash as Harry's accepts no known credit cards.

Performing Arts

Live theatre, concerts, ballets and operas also thrive in Sydney. Check the listings in the Friday and Saturday editions of the *Sydney Morning Herald* or the *Telegraph Mirror* for details.

The 'Halftix' (Monday to Saturday, noon–6pm) booth at Martin Place sells affordable reduced-price tickets for many performances (but only if bought in person, in cash and for that evening's performance).

Movies

The big cinemas showing first-release films are located in George Street (between Bathurst and Liverpool streets) and in Pitt Street (between Market and Park streets). Visit the **State Theatre** at 49 Market Street for its sumptuous art deco interior even if you don't care very much for what's playing inside.

Again, check Friday's *Sydney Morning Herald* entertainment supplement , 'Metro', or Saturday's *Sydney Morning Herald* to find out what's on. The **Valhalla** (Glebe), **Academy Twin** (Paddington), **Dendy** (Martin Place and George Street) and **The Village** (Double Bay) tend to show quality films (rather than the *Mutant Poltergeist Terminators 3* genre), while the **Hayden Orpheum** (Cremorne) is a restored gem of 1920s 'picture palace' architecture. There are also plenty of suburban cinemas.

Calendar of Special Events

Transport and hotel bookings are very heavy during the school holidays, so book well in advance. Be prepared for plenty of company everywhere, and for pretty slow business responses. Approximate times for school vacations are:

Christmas/Summer: mid-December to end of January.
Easter: 10 days over Easter.
Winter: Last week in June to second week in July.
Spring: Last week in September to second week in October.

JANUARY–MAY

26 January: Australia Day. Celebrates the arrival of the First Fleet in 1788. Public holiday, speeches, big fireworks, etc.
January: Festival of Sydney and Carnivale. A month-long programme of local and imported music and theatre, plus a big offering of multicultural events.
Late February/early March: Gay and Lesbian Mardi Gras. One of the biggest parades of its kind in the world, plus a huge dance party, all preceded by a season of gay art and theatre.
March/April: RAS Easter Show. The country comes to town in this huge expo of rodeos, woodchopping, cattle judging and sideshows.
April: Coca Cola Surfing Classic. Part of the world professional surfing circuit. Top surfers and good autumn surf.
April: Dragon Boat Festival at Darling Harbour.
April: Sydney Film Festival.

JUNE–DECEMBER

June: (even years) Australian Art Biennale .
August: (first Sunday) City-to-Surf Race. Thirty thousand runners compete in this race from the city to Bondi.
September: Rugby League and Rugby Union Grand Finals. Gladiatorial combat in the two codes of Rugby football.
October: Bathurst 1,000 saloon car race. This is the premier touring car race, televised live.
October: Upper Hunter Wine Festival.
26 December: Start of Sydney-to-Hobart Yacht Race. The harbour goes crazy as hundreds of craft try to witness (and avoid) the flying maxi-yachts starting in this blue water classic race.

The harbour is a hive of activity

Practical Information

fic. If you are departing from Sydney during the afternoon rush, allow up to an hour to get to the airport.

There are stands at all terminals for all the main rental car companies (Avis, Hertz, Budget, Dollar etc). The Travellers Information Service at the south end of the arrival hall at the international terminal can supply information and maps of Sydney and assist you in booking accommodation.

GETTING THERE

By Air

Sydney is Australia's major international gateway, serviced by flights from Asia, the Pacific, Europe, Africa and North America. Some 30 international airlines have regular scheduled flights to Sydney. Sydney is also well serviced by daily domestic flights.

Sydney (Kingsford Smith) Airport is located on Botany Bay, 9km (5½ miles) from the city centre. There are three terminals: the international at the western side of the airport, and the two adjacent domestic terminals of Australian Airlines and Ansett Australia.

Government buses operate regularly between the international and domestic terminals. Alternatively, take a taxi but ; will cost you more. Both can be found at the entrance to any terminal.

There is no rail link between the airport and the city. From all airport terminals take the yellow Airport Express bus (No 300 to the city and No 350 to Kings Cross) which takes about 30 minutes to reach the city and a similar time to Kings Cross. Both buses go via Central Railway Station. Alternatively, a taxi is faster but will cost about A$20.

Sydney's roads are quite narrow and are very crowded during peak hour traf-

By Rail

The terminal for all rail journeys into Sydney is Central Railway (known simply as 'Central') at the southern end of the city centre. However, nearly all city hotels are outside walking range (particularly if you are carrying heavy baggage) of Central Railway.

There is an adjoining electric suburban rail station with regular trains that travel to the city centre and the suburbs, but there are some flights of stairs to be negotiated. A taxi from Central Railway to downtown or a Kings Cross hotel will cost about A$5. Alternatively, there is a bus stop with regular departures to the city and suburbs.

By Bus

There is an extensive inter-state bus system and fares are cheaper than rail or air. Most of the bus terminals are on the fringes of the city centre. You will probably require a government city bus or a taxi to get to your hotel.

TRAVEL ESSENTIALS

When to Visit

Any time is fine, though obviously summer (December–February) is hotter, and winter (June–August) is colder and

windier. The seasons are the opposite of those found in the Northern Hemisphere. Spring (September–November) and autumn (March–May) are delightful times, usually with clear skies.

Visas and Passports

All visitors require a passport and visa to enter Australia, except for New Zealanders, who require a passport only. Visas are free and valid for up to six months. Applications can be made at the nearest Australian or British government representative. An onward or return ticket and sufficient funds are required.

To extend your stay, contact the Department of Immigration a month before your visa expires. Again you will have to show sufficient funds and an onward ticket. The maximum time, including extensions, allowed to visitors is a year. The Immigration Department head office is at 477 Pitt Street, Sydney, tel: 92197777.

Vaccinations

Vaccinations are not required if you are flying directly to Australia and have not been to areas infected by smallpox, yellow fever, cholera or typhoid in the 14 days prior to your arrival.

Customs

Visitors 18 years old and over are allowed to bring in 250 cigarettes or 250gm tobacco or cigars, one litre of alcohol and other dutiable goods to the value of A$400. A$200 worth of dutiable goods are allowed in the personal baggage of children under the age of 18.

Australia has very strict regulations on the importation of foods, plants, animals and their by-products. You will be safe to assume that almost anything of this nature will be confiscated at Customs. Heavy jail penalties apply to drug smuggling of *any* kind.

Australia is rabies-free and all incoming animals are placed in quarantine. The minimum period for cats and dogs – including seeing-eye dogs – is 6 months.

Weather

The wettest months are March and June, the coldest is July and the hottest are January and February. Mean temperatures are: summer 21.7°C (71°F); autumn 18.1°C (64.6°F); winter 12.6°C (54.7°F); and spring 17.4°C (63.3°F).

Clothing

For a summer visit, include a sweater or jacket to cope with the occasional cool spell. Also bring or buy an umbrella. Don't forget your swimming costume and sunglasses. A sunhat will provide protection against the harsh Australian sun, and a pair of good walking shoes is recommended. In spring and autumn, clothing should be light to medium weight. During winter, include warm clothing, a raincoat and umbrella. Though it never snows in Sydney, and it rarely gets below about 10°C (50°F), the weather can get really chilly.

In general, Australians are casual dressers, and lightweight comfortable clothes are ideal for Sydney. For dining at better hotels and restaurants, a jacket and tie may be required.

Electricity

The current is rated at 240/250 volts, 50 hertz. Universal outlets for 110 volt shavers and small appliances are usually found in leading hotels and motels. For larger appliances such as hairdryers, you will need a converter and a special flat three-pin adaptor to fit Australian power outlets.

Time Differences

Sydney operates on Australian Eastern Standard Time, and is 10 hours ahead of Greenwich Mean Time. It is 30 minutes ahead of Adelaide and Darwin, and 2 hours ahead of Perth, in Western Australia. Daylight savings operates between October and March when the clocks are advanced one hour to Eastern Summer Time.

GETTING ACQUAINTED

Geography

Sydney is located on the southeast coast of New South Wales. With a population of around 3.8 million people, it is the oldest, largest and liveliest city in Australia. It spreads over 1,736sq km (670sq miles), considerably larger in area than Rome or Los Angeles County, but the population density is a low 277 people per square kilometre. The harbour acts as a divider between north and south Sydney, with the city centre on the southern shore. The famous Sydney Harbour Bridge spans the bay to link these two areas.

Government & Economy

New South Wales' state government is run by a bicameral parliament (lower house Legislative Assembly and an upper house Legislative Council) which is elected every four years. Voting is mandatory for adults above the age of 18. Presiding over the state government is the Australian Federal Government in Canberra. Below the state government is a third tier of local municipal councils. No wonder Australians think they have too many politicians.

New South Wales has a healthy, mixed economy of primary industries (coal mining, wheat, wool, dairy, wine etc), secondary (steelmaking, manufacturing etc) and tertiary industries. Education, the arts, banking and insurance are major players in the state economy. Almost half of Australia's top 100 corporations are headquartered in Sydney. Tourism is a vital force, bringing in almost 1 million visitors to the city each year.

Population

As Australia's largest city, with a population of 3.8 million, Sydney's people reflect an enormous mixture of nations, tongues, creeds and colours. Almost one third of the people were born overseas, and the city continues to attract some 40 percent of the nation's new immigrants each year. Earlier waves of settlers from the British isles were supplemented by large numbers of post-World War II migrants from northern and southern Eu-

rope. Since the 1970s, there have been increasing numbers of Middle Eastern and Asian settlers, especially from Lebanon, Vietnam, China and Hong Kong.

MONEY MATTERS

Currency

The currency is the Australian dollar. Coins come in 5-, 10-, 20- and 50-cent, $1 and $2 denominations. Notes are $5, $10, $50 and $100. You may bring in or take out a maximum of A$5,000 (or its equivalent in foreign currency) in cash.

Foreign Exchange

Most foreign currencies can be cashed at the airport. City banks will change money between 9.30am and 5pm Monday to Friday. International-class hotels will change major currencies for guests. There are bureaux de change in some major tourist areas, but these are not found elsewhere, so it is best to change your foreign currency before an outing.

Credit Cards

The most widely accepted cards are American Express, Diners Club, Mastercard and Visa. In small establishments you may encounter difficulties with lesser known overseas cards. With any card problems, call:
American Express, tel: 98860666
Diners Club, tel: 008-331199
MasterCard, contact Thomas Cook
Visa, tel: 008-801256

Travellers' Cheques

All well-known international travellers' cheques can be readily cashed at airports, banks, hotels, motels and similar establishments. Offices of Thomas Cook and American Express are in the city centre. Encashment fees and rates of exchange vary between establishments.

Tipping

Tipping is not obligatory in Australia. However, a small gratuity for special service is appreciated. Hairdressers and taxi drivers do not expect to be tipped.

In restaurants, however, it is usual to tip waiters up to 10 percent (maximum) of the bill for good service.

Departure Tax

A departure tax of A$27 is payable by all travellers. It may be paid at a post office prior to departure or at the airport. Only Australian currency is accepted.

GETTING AROUND

Taxis

You can stop and hire a taxi wherever you see an empty one. The flagdown rate fee is A$1.85. Thereafter, it is 92 cents a kilometre travelled. Phone bookings cost A$1 extra. Smoking is not permitted in public vehicles, so ask your taxi driver first before you light up. Make sure the driver knows how to get to your destination, especially if it's a small street in an obscure suburb. If you have a complaint, take note of the driver's number – every driver has to display a photo and identity card – and cab number, then call the taxi company. The main taxi companies serving the inner city are:

Premier Taxis, tel: 98974000
Taxis Combined Services, tel: 93328888
Legion Cabs, tel: 92899000

In addition, there are two companies that operate water taxis on the harbour:
Aqua Cabs, tel: 99224252
Taxis Afloat, tel: 99553222

Urban Trains, Buses and Ferries

The Urban Transit Authority publishes a comprehensive map which shows Sydney's train, bus and ferry services. It costs A$1 and is available from news agents or from the Urban Transit Authority Travel & Tours Centre located at 11–13 York Street, where you can also pick up free timetables.

Trains

Sydney has an extensive electric train service and this is by far the quickest way to get around. The service is frequent, and all services can be connected at the City Circle underground system. Smoking is not allowed on board.

Buses

Extensive bus services are run mostly by the State Transit Authority, with the main terminals located at Circular Quay, Wynyard Square and at the Central Railway Station.

Distinctive red government buses

known as **Sydney Explorers** roam throug a terrific 20-km (12½-mile) circuit Sydney's city sights, and will let you o at any of its 26 stops with the option to rejoin the bus at any time later. In ad dition, your ticket allows you to ride fr on all other city buses throughout th same day. The Sydney Explorer leaves 20-minute intervals from Circular Qua from 9.30am to 7pm daily. The rou trip takes about 90 minutes to comple Purchase tickets either from the Ne South Wales Travel Centre (Castlereagh Street, tel: 92314444), or board the bus.

Alternatively, there is a blue Bor and Bay Explorer bus service that cov a 35-km (22-mile) circuit of the Easte Suburbs , including Double Bay and W sons Bay) and across to Bondi Beach.

operates daily from 9am to 6pm and the fares are the same as the Sydney Explorer. A combined two-day pass is also available.

The Sydney Pass allows you unlimited rides on the train, ferry or bus (including the Explorer or Tramway). It also covers the Sydney Ferries' cruises, including the Harbour Cruise, River Cruise and Harbour Lights Cruise. The cost of the Sydney Pass is $60 for 3 days, $80 for 5 days and $90 for 7 days.

For information on transport call the Infoline at tel: 131500 between 7am–7pm daily.

Ferries and Cruises

Ferries are by far the nicest way of getting around Sydney. They depart from Circular Quay, where the Urban Transit Authority issues free timetables. The longest regular ferry runs are to Meadowbank and Manly; the latter covers 11km (6¾ miles) in 35 minutes. The shortest ride is to Kirribilli and it takes 10 minutes, offering a panorama of the city skyline.

Ferry services are also available at the Royal National Park to the south and Pittwater to the north. The New South Wales Travel Centre (19 Castlereagh Street, tel: 92314444) has the necessary details. There are a variety of commercial harbour cruises, as well as lunchtime and supper cruises, such as Captain Cook Harbour Cruises, from Circular Quay wharf No 6. Departing morning, afternoon and night, the cruises include – along with the scenery and commentary – coffee, lunch or dinner.

Monorail

A monorail runs between Darling Harbour and the City. Flat fare is A$2.50, and the trains run every 5 minutes from 7am to 9pm.

HOURS AND HOLIDAYS

Business Hours

Retail hours are generally 9am–5.30pm, Monday to Friday, and 9am–4pm on Saturday. Thursday night features late-night shopping until 9pm. Restaurants, snack bars, bookshops and local corner stores are open till late in the evening and sometimes all weekend. Most businesses are closed on Saturday and Sunday. Banks are open 9.30am–4pm Monday to Thursday, and till 5pm on Friday.

The Kings Cross branch of Thomas Cook is open from 8.45am to 5.30pm, Monday to Friday, and from 8.45am to 1pm at weekends.

Public Holidays

All banks, post offices, government and private offices, and most shops close on public holidays, which are as follows:

New Year's Day 1 January
Australia Day 26 January
ANZAC Day 25 April
Good Friday (3 days) April/May
Queen's Birthday 2nd Monday in June
Bank Holiday 1st Monday in August
Labour Day 1st Monday in October
Christmas Day 25 December
Boxing Day 26 December

ACCOMMODATION

Sydney has a large number of hotels spanning the various categories, from deluxe to budget – with more opening all the time. The New South Wales Travel Centre (open Monday to Friday 9am–5pm) at 19 Castlereagh Street, tel: 92314444 operates a useful accommodation booking service – it will find you a place to stay at no charge. The recommendations on this list are mainly in the city and Kings Cross area. If you have a particular desire to be in a certain suburb, check with your travel agent or the Travel Centre. You can also book accommodation at the Travellers Information Centre, International Terminal, Sydney Airport (tel: 96691583). It is open daily from 5am until after the day's last flight has left.

Deluxe

A very well appointed room in one of these establishments can cost anything from A$230 to about A$450 (single or double) – but much better deals are available if you shop around first. Air-conditioning, private bathrooms, TV, direct dial telephones, large king size beds and minibars are standard in all these lavish properties. Most of them are less than 5 years old.

ANA HOTEL
176 Cumberland Street, Sydney 2000
Tel: 92506000
A grand hotel that opened at the end of 1992, this All Nippon Airways' hotel has views of Harbour Bridge and across Sydney Cove to the Opera House. A class act that's hard to beat.

INTER-CONTINENTAL
117 Macquarie Street, Sydney 2000
Tel: 92300200
Soaring out of the shell of the historic Treasury building in the business district, this 31-storey, 544-room hotel combines old world style and modern facilities.

MANLY PACIFIC PARKROYAL
55 North Steyne, Manly 2095
Tel: 99777666
Situated right on Manly Beach, the 145-room Manly Pacific is less than 30 minutes from the city by ferry and retains the relaxed character of a seaside resort.

MARRIOTT
36 College Street, Sydney 2000
Tel: 93618400
Facing Hyde Park, this new 255-room hotel has been highly praised for the quality of its rooms and service.

OBSERVATORY HOTEL
89–113 Kent Street, Sydney 2000
Tel: 92562222
Australia's first Orient Express Hotel, the 100-room Observatory which opened in February 1992, is the newest of Sydney's luxury hotels. In keeping with its pedigree, it is the last word in service, luxury and facilities.

PARK HYATT
7 Hickson Street, The Rocks, Sydney 2000
Tel: 92411234
Perfect location on Sydney Cove for its 163 rooms on four storeys. Incredible views keep this hotel near-full all year round.

QUAY WEST APARTMENTS
98 Gloucester Street, Sydney 2000
Tel: 92406000
Sandwiched between the Regent and the ANA, Quay West has the same grand vistas and 144 spacious apartments with complete kitchens and luxurious fittings. Facilities include a sauna, indoor pool, gym and room service.

REGENT SYDNEY
199 George Street, Sydney 2000
Tel: 92380000
This has been Sydney's best hotel for most of the past decade. Good location at Circular Quay and an impressive atrium foyer. 620 rooms on 36 floors.

RITZ-CARLTON
93 Macquarie Street, Sydney 2000
Tel: 92524600
Grand in the American classical manner – furnished in antiques and permanently burning open fires. A boutique-style with 119 rooms on 10 floors.

SHERATON WENTWORTH
61–101 Phillip Street, Sydney 2000
Tel: 92300700
For more than 22 years, an enduring part of Sydney's five-star hospitality scene. 465 rooms on 17 floors, frequented by regulars who appreciate its attentive service.

The Landmark, Potts Point

81 Macleay Street, Potts Point 2011
Tel: 93683000
A modern 472-room hotel with some excellent restaurants. The westward-facing rooms have Sydney's best views of the city skyline. This is a more relaxed area than adjoining Kings Cross.

The Renaissance

30 Pitt Street, Sydney 2000
Tel: 92597000
This flagship property of the Ramada group in the South Pacific opened in the business heart of Sydney in 1989. There are 579 rooms on 32 storeys, and four floors are for Ramada executive club guests.

Expensive

Priced between A$130 and A$230 per room (double or single), these hotels rate from three to four stars. All have direct dial telephones, air conditioning, TV/radio and en suite bathrooms.

Chateau Sydney

14 Macleay Street, Potts Point 2011
Tel: 93582500
In the centre of Kings Cross, this hotel has 96 rooms, a heated pool, barbecue and laundry.

Parkroyal at Darling Harbour

150 Day Street, Sydney 2000
Tel: 92614444
Opened in 1991 and overlooking Darling Harbour, this 295-room hotel over 10 levels takes full advantage of this recently developed part of town. It's only a short walk to the city.

Swiss Grand All Suite Hotel Bondi Beach

Campbell Parade, Bondi Beach 2026
Tel: 93655666
Overlooking the famous sands and surf of Bondi Beach, the Swiss Grand isn't far from the city. Plus, it is well located for the attractions of the Eastern Suburbs. Facilities include an excellent gymnasium and a pool.

Sheraton Sydney Airport

Corner of O'Riordan and Robey streets
Mascot 2020
Tel: 92351277
Opened in 1991, this 318-room hotel has double glazed windows and in-house videos for those wanting to rest; a heated pool and fitness centre for those who don't.

The York

5 York Street, Sydney 2000
Tel: 92647747
Situated very close to the Sydney Harbour Bridge, this property consists of 130 self-contained apartments. Features a heated pool, a spa and sauna, and laundry facilities.

Moderate

Priced from A$80 to A$130 per room (double or single), these hotels are comfortable and clean without being plush.

Park Regis

Corner of Castlereagh and Park streets,
Sydney 2000
Tel: 92676511
Boasting a good location in the centre of Sydney's shopping district, near the Town Hall, this air-conditioned 120-room hotel has TV, radio and direct dial telephones.

Victoria Court Hotel

122 Victoria Street, Potts Point 2011
Tel: 93573200
Boutique private hotel of 22 rooms, all with en suite bathrooms, TV, direct dial phones and a pleasant conservatory full of plants as a breakfast venue.

THE RUSSELL
143A George Street, Sydney 2000
Tel: 92413543
A 30-room two-storey boutique private hotel in The Rocks area. All rooms have direct dial telephones and rates include a large continental breakfast.

Hostels

Sydney has two city hostels operated by the Youth Hostel Association. The one at 262–264 Glebe Point Road, tel: 96928418, has 120 beds in 50 dormitories. The second, at 407 Marrickville Road, Dulwich Hill, tel: 95690272, has 114 beds in 57 rooms for long term visitors. A third, with 250 beds and a rooftop swimming pool, is at 51 Hereford Street, Glebe, tel: 96605577. Although it certainly isn't convenient for the city, the YHA hostel off Church Point on Pittwater provides a chance to inexpensively experience Sydney's bush, sun and saltwater lifestyle.

There are many privately run hostels in the Kings Cross area, particularly in Victoria Street. The Down Under Hostel, 25 Hughes Street, Kings Cross, tel: 93581143, is well run and good value, but occasionally gets overcrowded. The reception area has a notice board that offers items for sale, and useful tourist tips. The original Back Packers Hostel, 162 Victoria Street, tel: 93563232, has 150 beds.

Budget hotels are mainly located in the city, Kings Cross or Bondi areas. There is a 100-bed YWCA in the heart of Sydney – at 5 Wentworth Avenue, Darlinghurst, tel: 92642451. In the city is the Sydney Tourist Hotel at 40 Pitt Street, tel: 92115777. Directly opposite is the CB Private Hotel, tel: 92115115, with 200 rooms. In Kings Cross, the Gala Private Hotel at 23 Hughes Street, tel: 93563406, and Springfield Lodge at 9 Springfield Avenue, tel: 93583222, are worth a look.

Useful Numbers

In an emergency requiring police assistance or ambulance service, or in the case of fire, dial 000. Other emergency numbers: Crisis Centre, tel: 93586577; Rape Crisis Centre, tel: 98196565; Interpreter Service, tel: 91131450.

Security and Crime

Sydney is a relatively safe city, and you do not need to worry unduly about mugging or theft. However, take the usual precautions and don't tempt thieves. Avoid dark, empty lanes late at night in the city, don't leave your hotel room unlocked or money and other valuables unattended, and keep wallets and purses out of sight.

Medical

Hospitals and doctors are readily available, but overseas visitors are not covered by the government's Medicare policy. A visit to the doctor will cost A$35 and up. British passport holders are eligible for free basic emergency care at public hospitals, via a reciprocal agreement. A travellers' health and accident insurance policy is recommended for all visitors.

Pharmacies

'Chemists' or pharmacies have qualified professionals who dispense prescribed medication. They also carry familiar brands of general medications, cosmetics, toiletries, etc. Visitors are allowed to bring up to four week's supply of prescribed medications. For larger quantities, keep a doctor's certificate to avoid difficulties at Customs. There are a number of late-night pharmacies in the inner city area, mostly around Kings Cross: **Belgenny Pharmacobert**, Bourke Street, Darlinghurst. Tel: 93604959
Crown Street Pharmacy, 672 Crown Street, Surry Hills. Tel: 91697259

Dental

For dental emergencies, contact tel no: 96920333 or 96920598, or consult the Dentists section in the *Yellow Pages*.

Drinking Water

It is safe to drink water straight from the tap in any Australian town. If you prefer bottled mineral water, they're available everywhere.

Sunburn

The summer sun in Sydney is extremely strong. Wear a wide-brimmed hat to protect your face and avoid sunbathing between 10.30am and 3.30pm when the UV rays are strongest. Use a sunscreen with a high Sun Protection Factor.

COMMUNICATIONS AND NEWS

Post

Post offices are open 9am–5pm from Monday to Friday. In addition, the General Post Office (in Martin Place) is also open on Saturday mornings between 8.30am and noon. Post offices will hold mail for visitors, as will American Express offices for their card holders.

Telephone and Fax

Local calls from public telephone cost 40 cents for an unlimited time. STD (Subscriber Trunk Dialling) is for calling long distance within Australia. STD calls are cheapest between 10pm and 8am.

ISD (International Subscriber Dialling) is used for direct dialling overseas. ISD public phones are fairly common at post offices, airports and hotel foyers. Dial the access code 001, followed by the respective country code: France (33); Germany (49); Italy (39); Japan (81); Netherlands (31); Spain (34); UK (44); US and Canada (1). If using a US credit phone card, dial the company's access number below, followed by 01, then the country code. Sprint, tel: 1800-551110; AT&T, tel: 1800-551155; MCI, tel: 1800-551111.

To call Sydney from overseas, dial the country code 61, followed by the area code for Sydney, 2.

International-class hotels have business centres with fax machines, otherwise faxes can be sent from post offices.

Media

Sydney has two daily newspapers, the Sydney Morning Herald and the multi-edition Telegraph Mirror. The Financial Review and The Australian are national dailies. The Sydney Morning Herald is a must on Fridays when its green 'Metro' entertainment guide is included. Sundays are for the tabloids with the Sun-Herald and the Sunday Telegraph.

The Bulletin is a weekly magazine which includes the Australian edition of Newsweek. The Guardian Weekly, USA Today and the International Herald Tribune are on sale at most newsagents. Airmail copies of overseas newspapers and journals are available at specialised outlets in Kings Cross or Martin Place.

USEFUL INFORMATION

Tourist Information

Australian Tourist Commission offices provide plenty of advice and brochures for people visiting Australia. The head office is located at: Level 4, 80 William Street, Woolloomooloo, Sydney 2011. Tel: 93601111, fax: 93316469.

The New South Wales Travel Centre is located at the MLC Building, 19 Castlereagh Street, near Martin Place. The staff will make rail, coach, air and accommodation bookings for you, as well as provide information and brochures. The Travel Centre is open Monday to Friday 9am–5pm. Tel: 92314444.

The Travellers Information Service at tel: 96695111 (daily 8am–6pm) has advice on accommodation, tours, shopping, etc. The Sydney Convention and Visitors Bureau at tel: 92352424 shares a kiosk in Martin Place with the 'Halftix' booth (*see page 91*), and is a useful source of information. There is also an information booth at the western end of Circular Quay.

Sydney for the Disabled

Advance notice with relevant details of your disability will ensure that you receive the best assistance from airlines, hotels and railway offices. The New South Wales Travel Centre's publication, *Sydney Visitor's Guide*, details all the places that it recommends to disabled visitors. Cinemas and restaurants are happy to assist, although not all cater for wheelchairs. Specially outfitted taxis are available, but these must be booked in advance. Enquire at tel: 93390200. The Australian Council for the Rehabilitation of the Disabled (ACROD) can be contacted at tel: 98094488.

SPORTS

Sailing

Sailing is a popular pastime with many Sydneysiders. The yachting season runs from September to May. Races and regattas are held nearly every weekend.

Surf Carnivals

One is held at one of Sydney's ocean beaches on most Saturdays between October and March. The carnivals consist of swimming, surfboat and board-paddling events.

Surfboard Riding

In summer and autumn there are surfboard competitions. Listen for the morning radio surf reports on MMM-FM and JJJ-FM.

Yacht Races

Held every Saturday. The spectators' ferry leaves Circular Quay at 2pm. The start of the Sydney-to-Hobart Yacht Race on Boxing Day is a major sporting event in Sydney.

Golf

There are many public courses for the golfer. Check the *Yellow Pages*, then call the course club house for details.

Running and Jogging

Centennial Park, the Domain and Bondi Beach are popular spots for running or jogging.

Skiing

Ski season is between June and September in the Snowy Mountains, southwest of Sydney. Expect crowded slopes, fair snow and expensive accommodation.

Horse Racing

Sydney has six race tracks of which Randwick is the closest to the city. Races are scheduled throughout the year at Canterbury, Rosehill and Warwick Farm. Trotting races are held on Friday nights at Harold Park, and greyhound races on Saturday nights at Harold Park or Wentworth Park.

Rugby League

Games are played from March to September at the Sydney Sports Ground and at many suburban ovals.

Cricket

The season runs from October–March and international and interstate matches are spread throughout this period. Games are played at the Sydney Cricket Ground as well as suburban ovals.

Motor Racing

Eastern Creek raceway has regular car and motorcycle meetings throughout the year.

Aerobics

Dozens of gyms, such as Healthlands Fitness Network, City Gym etc, offer classes each day.

Others

Sydney has numerous public courts and private tennis clubs. Look in the *Yellow Pages* and call for details. In addition there are hockey, ice-skating and roller-skating rinks, gliding clubs, squash courts and more. Enquire at the New South Wales Travel Centre for more details.

USEFUL ADDRESSES

Airline Offices

Aerolineas Argentinas: Level 2 580 George Street, Sydney. Tel: 92833660
Air Caledonie International: Level 10 403 George Street, Sydney. Tel: 92678455
Air France: 12 Castlereagh Street, Sydney. Tel: 93211030
Air Nauru: Suite 502, 17 Castlereagh Street, Sydney. Tel: 92218622
Air New Zealand: 7th floor 90 Arthur Street, North Sydney 2061. Tel: 99574388
Air Nuigini: 100 Clarence Street, Sydney Tel: 2901544
Air Pacific: 1297 Pitt Street, Sydney. Tel: 92214511
Alitalia: 118 Alfred Street, North Sydney 2060. Tel: 99221555
All Nippon Airlines (ANA): 2 Chifley Square, Sydney. Tel: 93676711
Ansett Australia: Oxford Square, Sydney. Tel: 131300
British Airways: 64 Castlereagh Street, Sydney. Tel: 92583200
Canadian Airlines International: 1st Floor 30 Clarence Street, Sydney. Tel: 9251321, 92997843
Cathay Pacific Airways: 8 Spring Street, Sydney: Tel: 131747
Garuda Indonesian Airways: 55 Hunter Street, Sydney. Tel: 93349944
Japan Airlines (JAL): 201 Sussex Street, Sydney. Tel: 92689911
KLM Royal Dutch Airlines: 5 Elizabeth Street, Sydney. Tel: 92316333
Lufthansa: 143 Macquarie Street, Sydney. Tel: 93673850
Malaysia Airlines: American Express Tower, 388 George Street, Sydney. Tel: 32627
Olympic Airways: 37–49 Pitt Street, Sydney. Tel: 92512044
Philippine Airlines: 49 York Street, Sydney. Tel: 92623131

Polynesian Airlines: 50 King Street, Sydney. Tel: 92991744
Qantas Airways: 17 Hunter Street, Sydney. Tel: 99570111
Singapore Airlines: Singapore Airlines House, 17–19 Bridge Street, Sydney. Tel: 131011
Thai International: 75–77 Pitt Street, Sydney. Tel: 98440999
United Airlines: 10 Barrack Street, Sydney. Tel: 131717

FURTHER READING

General

Borthwick, John and McGonigal, David, *Insight Sydney* and *Insight Guide: Australia*. APA Publications, Hong Kong.
Issacs, Jennifer (editor), *Australian Dreaming: 40,000 Years of Aboriginal History*. Lansdowne Press, Sydney, 1980.
McGonigal, David, *Wilderness Australia: A Fragile Splendour*. Reed Books, 1990.
Morrison, Reg, and Lang, Mark, *The Colours of Australia*. Lansdowne Press, Sydney, 1982.
Raymond, Robert, *Australia, The Greatest Island*. Lansdowne Press, Sydney, 1982.
The Australian Adventure. Australian Adventure Publications, Sydney, 1987.
Wilson, Robert, *The Book of Australia*. Lansdowne Press, Sydney, 1982.

History

Barnard, Majorie Faith, *A History of Australia*. Angus & Robertson, Sydney, 1962.
Blainey, Geoffrey, *A Land Half Won*. Macmillian, Melbourne, 1980.
Clark, Charles Manning. *A Short History of Australia*. Macmillan, Melbourne, 1981.
Horne, Donald, *The Australian People: Biography of a Nation*. Angus & Robertson, Sydney, 1972.

Australian Language

The Macquarie Dictionary. Macquarie University, Sydney, 1982.
Wilkes, G A, *Dictionary of Australian Colloquialisms*. University Press, Sydney, 1990.

Index

Acknowledgments

Photography	**John Borthwick** *and*
Cover	**Dennis Lane/Apa Photo**
Backcover	**Adina Tovy/Apa Photo**
76, 94	**Stockshots/Roy Bisson**
36T, 45, 52B, 63, 75, 84, 90	**Stockshots/Geoff Brown**
66, 80B	**Stockshots/Phill Castleton**
36B, 69, 80T, 83, 87	**Stockshots/Myke Gerrish**
20B, 50B, 89,	**Stockshots/Graeme Goldin**
51	**Stockshots/M. Hall**
10T, 14, 19T, 22B, 30B, 31T, 31B, 35T, 35B, 39, 73, 101T	**David McGonigal**
29, 32, 44, 61T, 65B, 72, 74, 81	**Stockshots/Graham Monro**
92T	**Stockshots/Paul Nevin**
8/9	**Robbi Newman**
45	**Robin Nichols/Photobank**
38, 67	**Stockshots/Peter J. Robinson**
61B, 82	**Stockshots/Loreli Simmonds**
46, 65T, 77	**Stockshots**
10B, 71	**Stockshots/North Sullivan**
12, 30T, 33, 48T, 54, 68, 98	**Stockshots/Clifford White**
Handwriting	**V. Barl**
Cover Design	**Klaus Geisler**
Maps	**Berndtson & Berndtson**